RIPPLES OF *Positivity*

MOTIVATIONAL STORIES OF INSPIRATION AND POSITIVITY

RIPPLES OF POSITIVITY

First Published October 2024

Publisher: VISION BOARD QUEEN

ISBN:

Independently designed and published by the author.

Lisa Williams

www.lisawilliams-lmg.co.uk

Hosted By Lisa Williams

DEDICATION

To all the women out there who need to believe in themselves.

TABLE OF CONTENTS

INTRODUCTION

From as far back as I can remember I lived in a negative mindset. I wasn't aware of such a thing as a growth mindset, I also wasn't aware of personal development. It wasn't until I experienced several miscarriages that I was embodied in the feeling of being lost. I was in a dark place, with no self-worth, no confidence and feeling worthless as a woman; this was when I was introduced to this magical world of self-belief. I was finally given a magic wand to allow me to choose my future self.

Now don't get me wrong, it has not been an easy journey, but it has been one of magical moments. Moments that I would never have dreamed of several years ago. As part of my mission, I want to give others the power to choose, this book is jam packed with over twenty-eight stories. Twenty-eight incredible stories to create a positive ripple effect in your life and those around you. The reason behind twenty-eight has been studies illustrating evidence that 28 days can form a habit, I wanted to bring you twenty-eight stories of inspiration, motivation, and positivity to help you make small changes in your life.

I want these pages to become a tool kit of inspiration, motivation, and changes that you can use to help you on your journey of life. Life can throw us many challenges, some of which are harder than others to navigate. What I want this book to show you is that even with those challenges you can rise above them and move forward into a positive future.

Back in 2016 I was lost I had experienced my first miscarriage and held me and my body responsible for this loss, I never spoke about it, I TRIED to bury it. As I was suppressing this emotion, I was also self-loathing, self-hating and criticising myself for everything. Then when I went on to have a further miscarriage in early 2017, I was at rock bottom, I didn't have anything left to give, I knew I had to make changes. This was exactly what I did. I began to learn to love myself again, I was introduced to this magical world of personal development, I started to implement what I had learned from books, YouTube, and other people on the same path. I developed a toolkit to help me each day. In 2018 I again experienced another miscarriage; this time I had a toolkit there to support me. I knew I could get through this heartache as I had belief in myself. I no longer hated on me.

Since 2018 my toolkit has developed into a whole garage of tools that I can pull out when I need them, and believe me, I often need them. The more we grow and develop the more we accumulate new tools. I want this book to be twenty-eight tools you can use. Imagine using these twenty-eight chapters as a new motivational or inspiring tool each day that you can use to get through your journey.

And so, I welcome you to the collaboration and invite you to begin your journey through these twenty-eight chapters of tools and ripples of positivity.

CLAIM YOUR POWER

By Lily Rose

If you had said to me twenty-six years ago that I would be travelling over two seas, and have a business helping people discover themselves, I would have never believed you.

I was born in South Africa and lived most of my life there, then moved to Portugal to live with my parents to experience the way of life and culture there until the boys and I could move into our own place. Finally, my journey brought me to United Kingdom through work.

This is exactly what happened twenty-six years ago. I remember sitting in a little room with a psychic who read tea leaves, as I felt really stuck and did not know where to turn. Being married to an alcoholic was starting to take its toll on me. I remember her saying that I would be travelling across two seas. At the time it seemed unlikely, especially financially, and I just laughed, not knowing how that would happen.

I had two children who I adored, but I was stuck in a marriage which was killing me inside. It was not just the alcohol we had to endure, it was emotional abuse, controlling behaviour and people reporting back to him what I was up to. I was not allowed to talk to other men or even greet them at events when we went out. We did have a very socially active life, but I would always pay the price when I got home.

He however, had free reign and did exactly what he wanted, blatantly flirting in front of me with other women which made me feel worthless, unloved, and unwanted. I lacked confidence, and was a doormat, allowing everyone to walk all over me, even to my own detriment.

The universe started to work its magic, as on a very early morning around 6am, we were awoken by the distressed cries of the children and I discovered that the room that they were in was on fire. It spread so quickly that there was no time to put the fire out, we just had to get everyone out of the house. During the panic the baby who was two at the time, hid and we just could not find him. Three local police officers had just finished their shift and noticed the flames and came to our assistance. By this time the smoke had spread throughout the house they forced me out, and found my baby hidden behind one of the doors.

My ex was more concerned about his alcohol and not his child which really shook me, but at the same time, this was the catalyst that I needed to change my life. I started to plan how I could leave him to start a new life with the boys.

Afterwards it started to dawn on me, that all the memories, the pictures and everything else burnt up in the flames.

We momentarily moved into my parents in law's house until we could sort out insurance, which then paid out, which meant we could rebuild to our own taste, and this got me excited about redoing and redecorating the house from scratch.

At this stage I had not left him and continued to believe him when he said that things would change, and in my mind, there was hope and I trusted that it would happen, but this was not the case.

The house took months to rebuild, which I managed to do with a more modern look to the house and it really looked amazing by the time we moved in. We had a chance to build new memories.

I started to enjoy being in the house, but then something strange happened, and again with me being so naive I did not pick up on it.

A family member started to visit when I was home alone to 'check up on me' and started to bring gifts which he deemed as gifts for the house. In fact, what he was doing was grooming me to the point where he did say that if ever, I needed anything he would help me. And he meant anything. I did not put two and two together until he started to brush against me, or gently touch me. This really got uncomfortable. So, when he did just decide to pop in, I would just not open the door and finally told him that if he ever did that again I would mention it to my then husband.

Less than a year of us being in the house, there was an incident. My ex was drink driving and caused an accident. That evening, the police knocked on the door. This was just as traumatic for the children as it was for me, as he resisted the arrest.

When things settled, I started to look at the patterns, I decided that as things would never change, I did not want to subject my children to that ever again. So that day I started to finalise my plan of how I would make the change.

I managed to secure a flat, placed furniture in the flat, also had to plan to leave the house without his knowledge as I knew that he would have never let me go, but in part was afraid of what he would do if he knew.

In the middle of the day, I moved me and the boys to our new residence. That evening he came home to an empty home. This is when his behaviour became unpredictable and scary. He would be stationed at my place of work at start and finish times to either catch me, or to find out where we were living. I had to exit through the back door so that he did not know where to find us. When he figured out where we lived, he started to stalk us and I found out that we had no backing from the police, or even family who lived close by. Our only choice was to move out of the country. Divorce proceedings went ahead against his will and when we were finally divorced, arrangements were made for me to move to Portugal with my family.

It took us years to settle into our new lives free from the stalking, the emotional threats and abuse. My inspiration was my boys at every step of the way. I started to find myself again at my own pace. Making new friends, a new job, a completely new life. It was the first time I started to breathe again properly without having to watch my back all the time.

By the time I moved into my own place, the boys made new friends and were doing so well, I started to date again and had a friend who had also come out of a relationship and so we were there for each other, to comfort, to support and it really worked well for us. He helped me to start to see myself and helped me in more ways that I could have imagined.

I was doing so well with work that I was given the opportunity to move to the UK to work which I did for a few months, so the boys moved back in with my parents, in Portugal until I could afford to bring them over.

It was going so well until I was made redundant from a job which I really loved and excelled at. Again, the universe was steering me in a different direction. One which was more aligned with me and my soul path.

Being in the UK has taught me so many new things once again, and by the time lockdown started I was tapping into my spiritual gifts. I started to slow down completely and started to tap into the wisdom of my own body and gifts.

I trained in modalities like past life regression healing, angelic reiki, womb healing, shamanic healing, sound healing and tapped in more into essential oils and crystals, even was initiated as a rose priestess. Each of these was so powerful and profound. I also started to understand and heal some of my patterns, especially with the womb healing which I now support other ladies with. My work continues to evolve working with the most amazing energies to help and support those who are ready to take the journey.

My daily routine consists of a combination of the following: grounding, ceremonial grade cacao, practicing gratitude, meditation, sound healing, and listening to inspirational people who will lift me. I may use mantras, affirmations, crystals, essential oils. More importantly I tap into what I need that day and go with the flow. Tapping into my inner child from time to time is equally important.

There is so much advice out there about all the tools and techniques. What I would like you to do is to just pause a moment and feel into your heart space, feel what is right for you, or what your gut feeling is and go with it.

Looking back at my life over the last twenty-six years, there were times where I could not see a way forward, but I had this deep inner knowing and trusted there was so much more to life than what I was experiencing at the time. These lessons have brought me to where I am today, and they will always be a part of me.

Travelling over the two seas has also opened me up to my spirituality. In truth it has always been there, even as a little girl, but I never expressed it. As I open more to my soul gifts it allows me to live a more fulfilling life, in my sovereignty.

This has been a deeply transformational journey not only for myself, but also for those who I have had the honor to take through their own soul journey.

Finally, I would love to leave you with an ancient Hawaiian prayer called Ho'oponopono which I use, by placing your hands on your heart and say:

I'm sorry.
Please forgive me.

Thank you.
I love you.

ABOUT THE AUTHOR

LILY ROSE

Lily left an abusive relationship in 1998 to find a better life for both her and her two children. This journey took them to two different countries, finally settling in United Kingdom. In 2015 she was made redundant from a job she really loved, where she quickly spiralled into a depression.

In 2018, she trained as a reiki practitioner, and embraced her spirituality. During the pandemic, Lily was diagnosed with cervical cancer and invested more time into her spiritual journey training in past life regression, angelic reiki & womb healing. In business, Lily is passionate about helping women who feel exhausted with life and its demands, to heal and support them to find their own natural rhythm, predominantly through womb work which helps to bring back balance to their lives.

She also has vast first-hand experience on living with SEN children including the challenges and demands that come with it.

You can reach Lilly at:

https://linktr.ee/lily.rose.68

OVERCOMING ANXIETY AND EMPOWERING OTHERS.

By Nic Gray

My parents separated when I was five years old and at the time, I didn't realise it, but it was quite hard on me, and I started to struggle at school. All I ever wanted was to fit in. My earliest recollection of junior school was the fear of being bullied. We agreed that I would be better off moving schools at the age of about eight, which ironically was when my actual bullying journey started.

I felt like I wasn't good enough to have a stable home when I was younger, and I wasn't good enough to live a normal life, or a normal school life. That also led me to question all the time, 'am I good enough?' or to tell myself, 'I'm not good enough,' and as I reached adulthood and moved into the workplace, I realised that it had affected the career I wanted to go for too.

I had dreamt of becoming famous when I was younger and growing up I wanted to be an actress, or a singer. I soon realised that my confidence wasn't up to it. I then set my sights on becoming a teacher. I did my work experience at my old infant school but soon realised that, again, I 'wasn't good enough,' in my mind to become a teacher because I wasn't any good at science.

I look back and realise that if I found something too hard to understand I would simply avoid doing it as I didn't enjoy it. This has seeped into adulthood too but in a positive way. I now know what my strengths and weaknesses are in business and that I don't have to do it all.

Back then though, I knew that I needed good grades in English, maths, and science to be able to progress. So, after a rebellious year doing AS levels at sixth form college (and hardly attending any of the lessons!), I decided to throw myself into the real world.

When I was younger my grandad came back from work one day with a programme which he loaded onto his computer. It was a touch-typing programme. I was probably around twelve or thirteen and I would go to his house as often as I could and teach myself how to touch-type using this programme.

When I decided to head into the real world my first thought was office work. I went to a recruitment agency to see what jobs were on offer and they asked me what my typing speed was. By then I had a pretty good idea of the results I could achieve but they had a programme that told them the typing speed. I got straight to it, and they were very impressed with the ninety+ words per minute I could achieve at the young age of seventeen.

It wasn't long before I found a job as an office junior within an accounts department. This started my career in credit control, and I noticed as the years went by that my confidence grew when chasing businesses for payments and helping people come up with payment plans. Seeing great results and being good at what I did was taking me away from my earlier feelings of not being good enough. However, there were some bumps along the way, as I then periodically found myself the subject of office bullying.

When I look back at the bullying instances in the office, I feel like they were meant to happen to me. I have shaped my life on not treating people how I had been treated. It's where I learned love and respect for others. I never wanted anyone to feel the way that I had felt. I wanted to stand up for myself and others, but I still hadn't quite found my voice at this stage in my life.

I knew that I was good at what I did, I was getting the results and, in some cases, or in some places that I worked, there was no need to outsource debt to debt collectors as I was getting all the payments in. I knew my worth and I had to overcome the challenges of the office bullying which I believe often came from others not liking my good results.

I spent a lot of time during my life worrying about what others thought about me, all the time in fact. I was hardworking for fear of being told off and all I ever wanted to do was fit in. Towards the end of my employment, I could feel those fears starting to disappear. I could really feel that I was starting to gain some real confidence in what I was doing.

In March 2020 came the news of the global pandemic. I had to pick up my workstation and move it to my living room. I was also heavily pregnant with my second child and found the uncertainty of the pandemic extremely challenging. When I look back at those fears now, I realise that it really opened my eyes to the real world. I was seeing small businesses suffering left, right and centre and really started to appreciate the sentiment of truly shopping local. I would do all I could to help local business owners and leaving reviews for any purchases I made.

I spent the next three months working from home and really found that I could focus a lot better on my own. It was a big 'aha' moment for me. I've always worked better in a quiet space away from others and was really enjoying working from home. I had a great project to focus all my attention on and when my maternity leave had finally started and with the world the way it was, I started to get itchy feet.

During my maternity leave I went about trying out different types of businesses to see if it would be viable to either work in it part time alongside going back to work part time. Or whether I could find something that I could do from home around my children.

I started networking and built a huge love and respect for small businesses. During one of the last networking events, that I went to, before my maternity leave came to an end, it was suggested that I become a virtual assistant. This was something I had never heard of before.

Knowing that I really wanted to build my own small business and use my knowledge to support others, I was determined to make this business work. I went back to my employed job part time for the next four months, whilst building a social media following, networking, and advertising my business.

My breakthrough came in September 2021, one month after I set up my social media accounts. I had my first client, and by the December, I had the confidence to leave my part time employed role.

This was a huge milestone for me! I was finally growing up, not hiding behind anything, or anyone, and slowly gaining the confidence to not worry what others thought.

When I first started my business, I spent a lot of time reading, learning about social media and what I needed to do to be visible and grow my business successfully. I knew that to grow my business and make it a success I needed to overcome some of my earlier issues and thoughts of not being good enough.

I was determined, more than ever, that I was going to make my family proud and that I could empower others who had come from the same background as me that they could do anything too.

My mindset needed a lot of work, but the great thing about my newfound confidence was that I had surrounded myself with some incredible business owners and friends who are always there to lift me up and support me.

Through hard work and sheer determination, I'm growing a successful and award-winning business whilst raising a young family and I'm actually proud of myself. My goal now is to empower others, like me, to grow their own businesses too.

I began a VA mentoring course in January 2024 to become a VA mentor, rebranded in May, moved into my own office (in a room of my favourite café in Hailsham) and I am now preparing my first VA mentoring course to coincide with just over three years in business.

Sometimes I wonder, how did that young girl who lost her way, go from being bullied most of her life, thinking she had lost all her hopes and dreams to being this confident woman who owns her own business and is now recognised on the street and in networking meetings.

Could it be that all that she ever wanted had finally come true? Fame and teaching in a whole better scenario than she could ever have imagined.

Isn't it funny how they say, 'everything happens for a reason,' and it really and truly does.

If you've resonated with this story, even just a little bit, I really urge you to look back on your life today and piece it back together. Plan the future you always dreamed of.

I want you to know that whatever challenges you may face in life, you can overcome them when you believe in yourself and trust the universe. I didn't need to fit in after all, I just needed my halo to shine brightly.

ABOUT THE AUTHOR

NIC GRAY

Nic Gray is a devoted wife and mother of two daughters, and a Virtual Assistant and VA Mentor in East Sussex. Growing up she struggled terribly with bullies and always just wanted to fit in. Nic had always thought that she would grow up to be a teacher, but lack of confidence got in her way. She started her working career at age seventeen as an office assistant within an accounts department, became a Credit Controller and has forged a career in accounts and bookkeeping for some twenty years.

When her second daughter was born in 2020, during the Pandemic, Nic was diagnosed with post-natal depression and anxiety. She decided that this was her time to face those demons head on, come out of her shell, and start her own business.

Nic started networking in January 2021 and steadily built a very supportive following on social media. In August 2021 her virtual assistant business was born, and she soon became a multi award-winning business. One of her biggest highlights was when she was chosen by Theo Paphitis for his *Small Business Sunday Award* in November 2022 and got to meet the man himself twice in 2024.

Nic has a huge passion for supporting small, service-based businesses and uses her expertise in social media, email marketing, bookkeeping and administrative tasks to help others. Streamlining your business by handling the tasks you can't, wont, or prefer not to do. Your biggest business support.

You can reach Nic at:

www.facebook.com/nicgray.co.uk

UNBREAKABLE SPIRIT

By Emily Kent

Feeling the breeze blowing through my hair, the warmth of the sun beaming down on my face, as I sit at my favourite place in the whole world, the beach. Recharging myself, reflecting on life I sit and wonder how I got to this moment. Now I am at one with myself, at one with the waves as they almost flow in sync with every breath I take. A beaming smile, my heart filled with joy, is this reality? Am I dreaming? Can this be my life? I pinch myself almost in disbelief that this *is* my life, a life I felt was only in my dreams, one I yearned for many times yet never seemed to be in my grasp, you see my life unfortunately has not always been this perfect.

I felt from a young age that I was born into a world that I did not belong in. I longed to fit in, to be wanted, to be accepted. The *Black Sheep*, unloved and alone. My father left when I was just a toddler and little did I know that that was to be the end of our relationship. I spent much of my time with Granny growing up, she was my rock, the sunshine in my life, my safety net, although it was my safety net, it was also the place where I experienced one of the worst things in my life. We had many an adventure together. We lived with her for quite a few years and although my mum was there, I can't recall seeing her much, as a child; I never quite understood why at the time. We moved out from Granny's house and as time went on the family grew and I became a big sister, finally I wasn't alone but still always longed for affection and attention that I never received.

As the years went by, I turned to food to fill a void, it became my comfort, almost like a protection against the insecurities I felt within, lost, unloved and alone. I put on a brave face and tried to make the best of things as I could. Not really having anyone to talk to wasn't helping. My sister was somewhat younger than me. I adored her but almost felt a pressure to include her in everything that I wanted to do.

When I visited Granny, we would sometimes go to her neighbour's house. It was fun as we played games and sometimes his granddaughter would be there. There were a few times though when I was left alone with him and he would do inappropriate things with me, *our little secret* he would say. I felt numb and confused, unsure why this was happening to me. I felt trapped but desperate for attention. It didn't feel right, and I was scared but trusted him as an adult and thought it must be safe as I was allowed to go there. I wanted to tell someone to make it stop but was worried no one would believe me. My thoughts were so mixed up, I became very introverted.

As I got older, I realised this was not acceptable behaviour and I hated going to visit Granny as he would be there asking if I wanted to go over. At just eight years old I felt so vulnerable, confused, alone, afraid to say anything for fear I would get into trouble or worst still, hurt. This continued for a few years but thankfully the visits became less frequent, and I was able to get out of being alone with him, until one day something changed in me, I found an inner strength inside me. I told a friend that I needed to go to the phone box, and I called Childline.

I told them what was happening, and they listened to me, didn't judge me and for the first time I wasn't scared anymore, I felt BRAVE, COURAGEOUS, STRONG. I told my mum, and she supported me through it, I went to see a hypnotherapist to help me try to heal.

As I got older the pain became harder to deal with, I seemed to long for love and felt so insecure about myself, being bullied for many years for no apparent reason led me to become bulimic. For the first time in my life, I was in control of something. I could determine what I was eating and whether I was going to keep it down or not, it kind of gave me a sense of power, I was getting attention from my mum too which made me feel wanted.

I had so many hopes, dreams and aspirations for my future but unfortunately self-doubt and self-worth got the better of me. I fell pregnant at nineteen and had my daughter the following year. I felt like I had let my mum down but then that was the story of my life. My daughter brought so much joy into my life and even though I still had my own insecurities she gave me focus and a love I never felt possible.

My relationship with her father sadly was not meant to be. I met someone else a few years later, he was a real charmer, little did I know what I had let myself in for, I was completely gaslighted by this man and before I realised, I was powerless and trapped. He promised me the world yet destroyed mine. He belittled me, called me names, threw objects at me, lied to me, shouted at me, put me in debt, manipulated me and cut me off from my family. The only thing that kept me going in this situation was my daughter. I found out I was pregnant again and things didn't get any better in fact they got worse, he would go out and leave me for long periods of time, alone yet again in my life I longed for a way out. A way back to my family, a peaceful life for me and my children but it felt almost impossible.

One morning, out of the blue, he was arrested and taken away. I was unaware of what had happened; I didn't believe his fabricated tale and from that day forward, I prayed to God that there was a way out, hoping he would go to prison so I would be free, free from the abuse, the trauma that had become my life. Well justice was served he did go to prison, and I was finally free to rebuild my life. I started to take action.

There in front of me was the light. I was reconnected with my family, my friends and life finally felt like it was moving forward. I began counselling sessions and started baby steps in finding my self-worth again. Every day was a new day, a new opportunity to rebuild my life for me and my children, was it easy? Hell, no but I was not about to give up. Little by little things started to improve I started to find myself, surrounded by love from my family helped, I started to feel safe again. Although I still questioned life and wondered, 'why me,' I realised it was not my fault, no matter how much I tried I was never going to make sense of it all but that was okay, I had taken the hardest steps, and the worst was now behind me now. Finally, I had chance to breathe, to relax, waking up unafraid of what the day would bring gave me a sense of inner peace. My life was far from perfect, some days were still a struggle, but I was making changes and positive things were starting to happen. I found the confidence to get a part time job and make some new friends. Every day was an opportunity to learn and grow.

With each new day I started to believe in myself, appreciate all the good in my life, make small changes towards the life I deserved for me and my children, sadly I was faced with another tragedy when Gramps died suddenly. Down I fell, heartbroken and distraught yet again, all those old feelings of being alone washed back over me but this time I had to dig deeper than I ever had before. I started meditating with a beautiful lady and began to reconnect with myself from the inside. I began to find inner peace and reconnect with my inner child.

It took strength, determination, and resilience. It was then that my life started to really turn a corner, I met my now husband and we started our adventure together. We moved abroad to Spain, I felt a huge sense of release, a new opportunity for us all. We went on to extend our family and thoroughly loved life in the sun.

We returned to the UK as Granny became poorly and we wanted to be here with her. I am blessed to have spent the past six years making memories with her, but we sadly lost her this year. Although my heart is broken, I have learned that life is short so we must live for the moment and cherish everything. My goal is to continue to make her proud. I have an amazing relationship with my mum, she is my inspiration and the bond we have now is unbreakable. Long gone are those thoughts of not being wanted or loved. Time is a huge healer; it is important to remember this in our darkest hours.

Regardless of everything I have been through in my life it has never held me back, it's all about acceptance, never let anything stop you. The light inside will always guide us through even the darkest of days. Healing is a journey not a destination and is one which I will continue on through the next chapters of my life and beyond.

The POWER is within us all we just need to unlock it and believe in ourselves; I now believe in me, and I believe in YOU!

ABOUT THE AUTHOR

EMILY KENT

Emily is a dedicated beauty therapist with extensive experience in the industry, boasting over twenty years in customer service. As a qualified professional, she has honed her skills in making clients feel confident and beautiful.

In 2023, Emily ventured into the world of entrepreneurship by launching her online business, which specialises in selling lingerie. Her passion for helping women feel empowered and confident in their own skin drives her daily work. Outside of her professional life, Emily has a diverse range of interests. She enjoys walking, reading, socialising, travelling, and immersing herself in musicals. Her love for the arts has led her to participate in various performances and events over the years, showcasing her vibrant personality and willingness to take on new challenges. Emily's enthusiasm for life is matched by her commitment to giving 100% in everything she does, whether it's in her career or personal pursuits.

A proud mother of six, Emily considers her family her greatest achievement. She believes that raising her children has been her most rewarding and significant life experience. Emily is deeply passionate about supporting women in building their self-confidence and encourages them to believe in themselves. Her mission is to make a positive impact on the lives of others, helping them feel strong and self-assured. With a warm heart and a determined spirit, Emily continues to inspire those around her, both as a professional and as a devoted mother.

You can reach Emily at:

https://www.instagram.com/beautyandchills/

BACK TO BEING ME!

By Carla Draper

I was at home when I got the worst news I could get, my dad had a brain hemorrhage. He died a couple of days later, my body went to jelly, and I felt that my world turned upside down, I was due to get married eight weeks later and I didn't know what to do.

My friends and family around me supported me and said my dad would want me to still get married. I knew that it was the right thing to do, so I went into wedding mode and got married. It was a perfect day; I had my two boys, George, four and Jack, eighteen months with me and my eldest brother gave me away.

As time went by life as a mum and wife continued but day-to-day life got harder. My boys needed a lot of attention, I had housework to do and felt everything was down to me and my husband Robert didn't do anything. I started to feel down and lose my identity. I couldn't do anything right! Nobody was grateful for what I did!

Depression hit and I felt worthless, negative thoughts took over, 'My boys would be better off without me... my friends and family wouldn't miss me if I wasn't around.'

I felt like I wanted the room to swallow me whole, I just cried uncontrollably I wanted to end my life but deep down, I knew it was a cry for help! I got the help I needed with antidepressants for six months and counselling from Cruise, a bereavement counsellor.

Robert and I started talking a lot more and getting on better, working together as a family.

When I had down days, I opened up more to Robert and friends. I felt wanted and needed more, life had a purpose again. I was a mum of two boys who needed me to look after them. I knew my husband loved me for being me and I didn't need to change.

Looking back on this stage of my life I know now that as much as I miss my dad, losing him made me a stronger person today. I believe I can do anything I want to if I desire it enough. I live life to the fullest as much as possible and every day I encourage my boys that they can do what they want, to seize everything they wish however difficult it may feel.

Over the next couple of years, we bought an old stable that we converted into our home. I loved the new village we lived in; the boys went to school in the next village, which was a lovely school, and I made some good mum friends. I got myself a part time job at a local preschool that fitted perfectly with the boy's school hours.

In 2018 I started running which was a great release of stress, a good bit of fresh air and a great way to start the day. Then my upper back started to hurt every time I ran, and suddenly, my neck, shoulder and upper arm hurt continuously. The intense pain meant daily chores were difficult, I couldn't use my right arm for long periods of time. I had an MRI scan which showed I had a bulging disc in my neck.

In the summer 2019, after a day at Legoland I woke up with bad lower back pain. Again, after an MRI scan, I had a bulging disc at the bottom of my back.

The excruciating pain in my neck, shoulder, arm, and lower back led to me leaving my job. I was back in that black place, I didn't feel like Carla again, I couldn't do anything.

As the pain got really bad the doctor put me on the pain clinic waiting list to have a steroid injection but COVID came along, everything closed, and we all got put into lockdown.

I hated lockdown, home learning wasn't easy, my husband didn't really help much with schooling and the boys weren't too willing to do the work. When the second lockdown happened, Robert went back to work, Jack was able to go to school and George was able to get on with his work by himself. I felt very lonely, no one to talk to, each day felt the same.

I still tried to feel positive and put on a brave face, but it really wasn't easy.

In summer 2021 the world opened back up; things went back to how we knew it. This meant hospitals were open again and I was finally back on the list for the steroid injection.

I had months in pain, no work, feeling useless again and depression was bad again. Robert and I had lots of silly arguments then one day we had another one and I hit rock bottom, I wrote a suicide note and took a small overdose again. I cried and cried and cried, Robert called an ambulance and I saw the crisis team at the hospital. When I came home from the hospital my family hugged me and let me know that everything was going to be okay.

I was diagnosed by a doctor that I had severe depression, got put on anti-depressants and on the waiting list to see the crisis team for some one-to-one help. I didn't have to wait too long for these, they helped a lot, and we dug down into childhood memories. I opened up a lot, shared things that I didn't know were upsetting me at the time, it was such a relief, a weight had been lifted off my shoulders.

I was starting to feel better and home life was beginning to feel more normal.

I was back doing Pilates, seeing friends, and enjoying doing things again. After some time, I finally had the steroid injection in my lower back which was a God send for me. I was pain free, I could move like myself, I was Carla again!

Just before COVID I joined ‘The Body Shop at Home’ which meant during COVID everything went online including networking. In a networking session I joined a vision board group, I got so much out of it. I’m still part of the vision board group today, it inspires me to be the person I am today.

Through doing the vision board I realised that ‘The Body Shop at Home’ wasn’t for me, and I needed something else for me. I discovered that I had let go of mum guilt and that taking time for me was essential. Finally, I had the self-belief that I could do something that I enjoyed but the question at the time was, ‘What?’

Robert and I had a small argument over nothing, which meant I ended up at Costa having a cuppa with a friend, this was where my light bulb moment came... I wanted to BAKE!

September 2022, George was thirteen, in Year 9 and Jack eleven had just started secondary school. I had extra time on my hands with no more school runs, which was bliss, I was in a good place, and I could venture out and start my own business.

‘Carla’s Everyday Bakes’ was born. I knew that I didn’t want to bake the big birthday cakes, wedding cakes and cupcakes. I knew loads of people did those and I wanted to do something different.

Traybakes was the way I wanted to go, I wanted to make simple cakes. But how did I get my name out there? I made a Facebook page; I shared this and invited my friends and family to join the page. I had a launch day at my house, a chance for people to sample and buy my bakes.

Next, I started to fill my diary with Christmas fayres and fetes, I knew these were going to be hard to judge how much to bake but I had to get my name out there. I was over the moon when people bought from me.

It was hard work at the start, but I had so much support from my friends and family who had faith in me, so I kept going. In January I had my first weekly order from a local café, this gave me a constant income, I was feeling so proud.

Over the summer I did the summer fetes and by then knew how much to bake and not to worry if the cakes didn't sell. My mindset was good, I was feeling very positive. Year one had passed so I celebrated with a party.

I moved my business forward by providing for another café in the village, I was getting a proper income, which meant I didn't need to book as many fetes as the previous year so I could spend weekends with my family.

I have now entered my 3rd year in business and I am known as 'The Cake Lady.' I still get back pain, down days but these are few and far between. I have achieved so much and learned so much about myself, I am a much better person than I was over ten years ago.

I am really looking forward to the future, seeing how far I can grow and what I can achieve.

I can now leave a legacy for my boys; they have grown up watching me start and be successful with my cake business. Hopefully this has taught them that you can achieve anything you want to do; you are worthy to go and achieve your dreams.

ABOUT THE AUTHOR

CARLA DRAPER

Carla, wife, and mum of two teenage boys, first started her business in September 2022 as both boys were no longer in primary school.

Carla wanted to do something for herself, something that made her Carla!

Baking was something she really enjoyed so she followed her gut and did something she was passionate about.

'Carla's Everyday Bakes' was born and now in its third year she successfully provides two local cafes weekly and is now looking for a third.

In 2013 she suddenly lost her dad, only eight weeks before she got married. Her life crashed down in front of her. She built herself up with help from friends and family.

In 2018 Carla suffered with a bulging disc in her neck followed by another one in her lower back a year later. She lived in agonising pain for years before getting any help.

Yearly she now has the nerve burnt which gives her a pain reduced life.

After joining a vision board group in COVID time she learned a lot about herself, this is where she learned how to let go of all the things holding her back, and realised how much she is worth. She is still part of the vision board group, where she has met a lot of wonderful ladies who have become a great support group to her.

She feels so blessed to be where she is now, becoming a better version of who she was and feeding everyone with CAKE!

You can reach Carla at:

https://www.facebook.com/carlaseverydaycakes

SOMEWHERE, SOMEWHEN, SOMEHOW

By Kez Adey

Leaving the house that morning, I didn't know where I was going, all I knew was my son was with my dad, he was safe. I decided my time had come.

I parked up and messaged a family member to tell my son, I love him. I put my phone down and all the f*ck ups flashed before my eyes. His face and voice haunting me, confirming I was worthless and miserable. My mind became full of anger towards the men who I thought had destroyed my life. One whose face and voice continually haunted me, the other, the surgeon who used my spinal column as a pin cushion. With my anger aimed towards anyone, mood swings, selfishness. The voice again told me everyone would be better off without me, this echoed around my head, the decision was made. It was time to end everyone's misery!

Sh*t, who rang the police? I didn't even think the police would be looking for me, I couldn't speed off, so I put the window down to talk to him and as he started to ask me if I was okay, my passenger door opened, and a family member stepped in. I was escorted home by the police then off to the hospital for six hours, to be discharged and told to wait for mental health services to contact me. More waiting around with no answers, feeling lost in a very crazy world not knowing what was happening, why the voices were getting louder and the night terrors were becoming more vivid and all I was being told was to wait.

Five weeks of waiting, during which the voice got worse, I'd be asleep and then out of nowhere his fist would come flying towards my face, waking me in shock. I went to the meeting and explained everything, their response whilst I sat there shaking was that I had post-traumatic stress disorder (PTSD) that had been caused by years of abuse. This didn't make sense as we hadn't been together for YEARS and he was no longer in our lives. I was left in the room alone for a further, twenty minutes, this seemed like a lifetime. Alone, with nothing but his voice telling me I should have done what I aimed to do that day. The nurse returned and gave me more tablets to take on top of those I already take and then came the words that would haunt me, "Your trauma is too deep, and we are unable to help you as you need specialist help."

WHAT, WHY, HOW? Yet again I was left alone with the voice in my head, his fist in my sleep and no support available, private counselling was out of my budget. So, I went home to try and explain why I'm always argumentative and moody.

Five years prior to wanting to end my own life I had gone for an operation to repair a slipped disc in my back. What I thought would be a simple procedure was much more complex, the operation took three hours longer than expected, finding this out once I was back on the ward was scary, why had it taken longer? What had happened? Had more been done than planned? There I was all night, no answers, the only time I saw someone was just to pump the morphine round and tell me I'd have answers tomorrow. The following morning, the doctors did their rounds, and I was ordered to take bed rest at the hospital with no explanation, no answers and no idea what was happening, Why or What had gone wrong? I was left confused and anxious as to why I couldn't walk without severe pain after what I had expected to be just a normal procedure and allow me to be an active mum like I wanted to be.

The doctors ignored my questions and I felt unheard. Five days later, I was still hospitalised with no answers of what the future held and left with chronic pain which resulted in needing to use a wheelchair.

I was discharged from hospital to care for my eight-year-old son alone, with no support. My ex's voice was louder in my head, it had been there since before my PTSD diagnosis but it was becoming louder and louder. Not only was I deemed a failure, but I was also not being the mother I wanted to be. The sound would always be there whether it was humming, talking, shouting, or even screaming at me that I was a failure to everyone especially my son, he didn't care where I was, he'd just be there all the time. ENOUGH WAS ENOUGH, it was time for me to make a difference.

I started demanding answers around my surgery. I learned that things would not get any better and I would always live with chronic pain, my legs constantly burning, although I can't feel anyone touching them. This screwed with my head even more because surely if I couldn't feel my legs, I wouldn't be able to walk, how would I cope?

My hips felt like they were trying to escape through my skin, often using a wheelchair. This was my life now, I felt so worthless and the downward spiral began, the self-hatred was taking over. I was a mess. Then came the devastating news, that I would never work again! I was twenty-nine and would never be able to support my family, being supported by the benefit system, people would presume I was just a scrounger.

In 2017 when I finally got the PTSD diagnosis, it changed my life, everything started to make sense, I finally felt like I had answers to my moods and anger, my life was changing, and it was down to me to decide how it would change my life. I finally started to open up about my story. I was very fortunate to have been introduced to a psychologist through a friend who offered to help me. I began this journey over two and half years every Wednesday. Initially I hated these sessions as they had control over my head, the hate thoughts, the plans of ending things. Eventually over time it helped. I found a sense of healing. I was now a survivor of the domestic violence I had previously suffered. It was abuse at its worst physical, mental, sexual, financial, coercive, and controlling and after ten years, I was finally in control of my thoughts.

After two years of therapy sessions, I had less noise in my mind. I finally felt lighter and relieved, I had control again and it felt like my life was my own again. When COVID-19 hit the UK, my mindset was in a much stronger position. I was put in a strict lockdown due to asthma that it was not safe for me to leave the house. I realised my help was needed in the community more than the risk of me getting COVID if I was careful.

Eventually lockdowns, news bulletins, Captain Tom and face masks were becoming a thing of the past and COVID restrictions were coming to an end. That's when the government announced they were closing most day centres. Day centres to most are just somewhere old people go. For many day centres are the only human contact that some people get, whether disabled, elderly or just in need of company. After two years of many seeing people in fleeting glances, no one sat down to have a cup of tea with them or just a gossip and now there was nothing to look forward to as their day out once a week or month was now gone, that gave me power, the fire in my belly to say enough was enough and someone needed to stand up for those that the government bullied daily.

I was beginning to see a new future; my purpose was to make my home city accessible for all. It started with a local councillor telling me disabled community would have to wait! WHAT, WAIT? This was outrageous, I felt like we had already waited long enough for changes to be implemented to help life be more accessible. In 2010 the Equality Act came into force, and this gave disabled people the belief that people cared; people were listening to us, but this had failed. The time had come that it was time to beat my anxiety and meet with councillors to discuss issues in their wards, council officers and many others to point out the issues that affect our lives daily. It was tough going but I felt the passion growing. I beat my PTSD and the voices in my head and believed I could!

'Disability Interest Group in Salisbury' was born. The first meeting came, and I was nervous. I walked out my door and back in so many times allowing the voices, my anxiety, and my PTSD to win, 'NOT NOW!' I said to myself. I went to the meeting expecting no one to be there, but oh my god, there were fifteen people who wanted to make a difference. We started bi-monthly meetings, meetings with professionals and suddenly people started listening to us. We branded ourselves as a group of people with a wide range of disabilities, we are making a difference.

We were listening to those who had felt left out of communities, decisions and so much more that impeded them living an active, social life that many wanted too.

We are now two years in, my PTSD is still here although I have control over the voices, most of the time, they are still there occasionally, my mental health is still a daily struggle and some days I can cope but others are not so good. On those days, I curl up in my chair, watching old films, cheesy TV, with a box of tissues, chocolate with lots of coffee and fizzy drinks. My pain levels are very high and I manage that with daily painkillers, I still often use my wheelchair because if I don't I will spend time in bed possibly for days due to the pain taking over. My anxiety is still waving at me, but I am able to walk out the front door without walking back in, I can meet with businesses and discuss accessibility and work with disabled people, although many people don't see the phone calls I make to believe I can do this and why?

I want to change the country for all those out there that need to be listened to too and that's because I know what it's like to be alone, not listened to and unimportant. After all, everyone deserves to live the life they wish to.

ABOUT THE AUTHOR

KEZ ADEY

Kez is a mum and step mum to two grown up children. Since having a failed spinal operation in 2013, Kez has been an ambulatory wheelchair user. Kez is a Disability Champion in her local area in 2022 and has built herself up to also become an accessibility coach to local and national organisations. They help organisations of all sizes to expand their profits by making their business all inclusive.

Kez works with a team of people with a wide range of disabilities to give businesses a real-life view on how inclusive their business is, whether that be their premises, website, or any other assets they have. Whilst doing all this work, Kez has worked on herself to believe in herself, her mental health, now managing PTSD as well as her mobility issues and chronic pain.

In 2023 'Play for Everyone' was launched by Kez and the team behind Disability Interest Group and they are now working on gaining recognition as a national charity whilst also helping organisations to be all inclusive for clients and employees.

You can reach Kez at:

www.facebook.com/groups/businessaccessibilitysupport

CAN YOU SEE ME?

By Lisa Matthewman

No really, can you see ME?

Singing has always been a huge part of my life. I can get up and sing in front of hundreds of people and not be phased. I have loved the music, costume, and drama from being a little girl.

Underneath I used to be shy and very, very insecure, my beautiful daddy used to call me a shy extrovert. In the past people would assume I was outgoing as they would see me on stage singing, however, in a room full of people I just wanted to fade into the background, it was crippling. Now I'm much more confident and will chat to new people, do I still have insecurities? I absolutely do, but these days I'm able to use the nerves and let them work for me rather than against me.

Lights camera action

For most of the time when I was onstage, I could play a character. Often the character was the version of me that I wanted to be. I worked at holiday parks as an entertainer for twelve years. Onstage I was larger than life, singing, dancing, running competitions, we joked that when we finished work you would get home at night and look in the mirror and the smile was still there, you couldn't switch it off no matter how tired you were, that was your persona!

'Eyes, teeth and tits,' was our saying, no matter how you were feeling, 'The show must go on.' I flipping loved working the holiday parks, it was hilarious and crazy fun. But during that time, there were also some heart-breaking moments. I met my first husband and had our two children but we soon split up. I should have seen it coming, he came out as gay some years later.

It was hard being a single mum, but with my parents support I picked myself up and continued to work in entertainment as a cabaret singer. Dad and I would go off to some strange little workingmen's clubs across the midlands and I would sing for the night, Dad was my roadie! We had an absolute blast together.

In the Gutter

During this time, I met my second husband, we were wrong for each other, but somehow ended up getting married. When I announced we were together my friends were gobsmacked and couldn't believe it, they might have been surprised but were always supportive.

At the time it seemed the perfect thing to do, we were running a recording studio, performing together, running a karaoke company, touring pantomimes – oh yes, we did! But my inner fears were right, and we weren't right for each other. He was working away and had an affair. We muddled through together for a few more years, but it felt so wrong, spending more time arguing, particularly about money.

It was a very dark time; debts had been run up on the music studio and put against my house. We entered an IVA paying money regularly to the company running it, but unbeknown to us they were crooked and hadn't been paying off the debts, we were taken to court and made bankrupt – I was absolutely devastated.

I thought that was it, we wouldn't be able to run our businesses anymore, the house was taken, I wasn't even sure how we were going to feed the kids. I can vividly recall driving home along the A14 behind a lorry, and thinking I could just put my foot down and crash into the back of that lorry and it really wouldn't matter. Thankfully the thought of the children kept me going.

Having a second failed marriage broke me. I felt stupid, how was I managing to get this all so wrong, not just for me but for the children, the second male in their lives deserted them. Their dad didn't have anything to do with them and now the guy who had taken a major role in their upbringing had gone. I just wanted to crawl into a dark space and sob.

I was back to being a single mum, renting back the house I had once owned. I didn't know how to keep going. I remember walking to pick the kids up from school and just sitting in the gutter sobbing, a stranger literally picked me up and led me to the doctor's where I was given help for severe depression.

Whilst all this was going on, I was running music sessions and my choir with a smile. That 'eyes, teeth and tits,' philosophy didn't go away; I was good at masking. To the world I was Miss Positive, inside I was crying.

I was predominantly working for Youth Music and running early years music sessions for them, however the hub I was working with, was taken over by some unscrupulous people, who ran it into the ground and lost all its money. I was left being owed £3k which left me at rock bottom.

Sink or Swim (or sing)

At that point it was sink or swim. I knew I had to face my fears, speak to my music venues directly, I couldn't be shy about this, I was determined not to go under. I had to be brave, proactive, get out of my comfort zone and explain what was going on with the company.

I'm so grateful they believed in me and my work and allowed me to continue working with them and to flourish. Through this I learned that I am very resilient and when I put my mind to something I have the courage and strength to tackle what needs to be done. My 'Music and Movement' business grew, and life got back on track.

I also had my fantastic choir, I started in 2008 and still going strong, music and singing is so uplifting, great therapy and good for the soul. Raising my voice with my fabulous choir ladies is such a boost every week.

When COVID hit, my music business almost stopped but I was not about to be beaten again, so I took both my choir and music sessions online. These fun musical moments helped keep my passion alive and stopped me going potty.

Once we were back making music in person the choir achieved some grants to help rebuild, the dedication of the committee and 'Big about Singing' members is so humbling. I'm forever indebted to them and incredibly thankful for all they do to support me.

The Show really does go on

I met Keith fourteen years ago and we have now bought our own home which we love. Together we are renovating. I ticked a big goal off my vision board and have a purpose-built office in the garden which is my happy place.

I'm lucky to have some wonderful lifelong friends who are always there to make me smile and help me, no matter if we see each other every week or once a year, when we get together it's as if no time has passed. We laugh, hug, chat, and sing.

I run an extra business with my daughter Sapphire. 'Elegant Essences,' we fell in love with the fragrances and sparkle of Scentsy following a party and we have now grown a fabulous business and amazing team. Seeing our team grow and promote is a joy and a privilege and when I'm smiling and talking about positivity, I really do mean it.

Running my businesses have built my confidence, my resilience, I know that I can face hard decisions head on.

With Keith I discovered a love of motorbikes, first going pillion, then I passed my CBT and spent months mastering riding, it wasn't easy for me. I nearly gave up, but finding the right bike, lots of encouragement from Keith and sheer tenacity and determination (as I really don't like to fail) at forty-eight I passed my motorbike test. Nine years on going out for a blast on Poppy, my Kawasaki Vulcan and having some wind therapy is almost as fun as singing!

Since hitting the menopause I've struggled with brain fog. I joined a menopause membership and went on HRT; both these have helped me with the symptoms. I'm trying to get fitter and healthier so I can continue to enjoy the life I have built. I now do a lot of walking; Keith often gets dragged out with me round the local parks and countryside. I feel so much better for it, and it not only helped me to lose weight but is great for my mental health.

I have three beautiful grandsons from my son, who I see every week, we play, laugh, make music together, I'm so very blessed to have them.

I have worked hard for the life I have now achieved, and I also get to play be it riding motorbikes, playing with grandchildren, relaxing in the garden, and drinking coffee with my fabulous friends.

That shy girl often creeps back in, and I do suffer with imposter syndrome and self-doubt, but I can rise above it, put my big girl pants on, (those Bridget Jones knickers), pull them up and get on with it, the smiles and encouragement and positivity are very, very real.

I am a strong believer and take pride in self-development. Over the years I have participated in various music courses for music work. Recently with the addition of the 'smelly' business I have focused on entrepreneurial courses and network marketing which has been inspirational and motivational.

I am so grateful for the life I have and the journey it took to get here, I don't take any of it for granted.

I am the Singing, Motorbiking, Scentsy Nanny!

#singingscentsylady

ABOUT THE AUTHOR

LISA MATTHEWMAN

Lisa is a mum, nanny, cat mum.

Lisa has always been involved in singing and music, from an early age she was performing in local shows. Going to college and studying drama for two years in Northampton. From there she auditioned to be a singer for Haven Holidays. That led to twelve years working holiday parks as a singer, entertainer, and entertainments manager.

Out of summer season Lisa auditioned to play the lead in a touring pantomime, touring round South Wales and the West Country. Lisa went on to start her own pantomime company StarrStoppers which toured round the Midlands putting on pantos in Clubs and Schools.

She had her own cabaret show which she toured round the midlands for over twenty years as Lisa Starr. During this time, she also performed as part of a duo – Maid two Measure and ran a Karaoke Company.

For the past twenty years Lisa has focused more on teaching than performing. She runs very successful 'Music and Movement' classes for children under five, also working with children and adults with additional needs and she runs 'Big About Singing' - Corby community choir who perform around the county.

Lisa takes self-development very seriously and has partaken in music courses to enable her to better her musical practice being one of the first four to gain the certificate for music educators in early childhood with Trinity College London. With her daughter, Lisa runs Elegant Essences Independent Scentsy consultants.

You can reach Lisa at:

www.facebook.com/elegantessences

THE VOICE THAT TELLS YOU TO "CARRY ON"

By Clare Gould-Smith

Looking back my self-esteem had always been low, mainly because of been bullied for most of my school years. I always had the feeling of not being good enough. Life and its trials have taught me the opposite, my new positive life has helped me create the creative life I always wanted.

I knew I'd always wanted a creative life, but life literally got in the way. Whilst at university doing my Art degree, I witnessed my first experience of how adult life can change in an instant. I saw my then partner stabbed and almost die before me, this certainly made me grow up overnight, thinking back now that probably was the first thing that tested my strength and that unknown voice saying, "You have to carry on."

After university, life, jobs and first homes, got in the way of being able to create the creative life I dreamed of and my life was rocked again more than I'd ever thought possible when in 2003 my dad suffered a stroke and died a week later, with no time to really say goodbye. Even though I was the youngest of five children I felt I had to carry on and help everybody else. I felt I needed to be the leader, to be the one to get everyone through, pushing my own grief away. This eventually led to a break down, as I had never let go or processed it properly. This was when I had my first encounter with spirituality, seeking help through hypnotherapy and reiki that I believe saved my life.

The only good thing at this time was meeting my husband, he was and is still now my rock, he helped me find what I needed to get better and a few years later we were blessed with our daughter. I began working for a large company doing something completely different, but not long after starting, I also lost my mum, something else to rock our world.

In my new career I did well and received a top award with the first eighteen months. I had been there for eight years when lockdown happened, and it gave me time to stop and revaluate. Finally, I had time to be creative again and I loved it, it made me feel alive. During this time, I also set up my gifting business which gave me that creative outlet.

Everyone started going back into the world, but I stayed home, I was working from home but being alone gave me more time to think, I've never been too good with time to think, I like being busy. There was no real structure or plan, I did not know what I was doing I was just playing so I started to feel like I'd failed that I wouldn't be any good, that I'd never make a go of it.

I started to doubt myself and my business and those negative voices filled my head. 'Who was I kidding, I was in my late forties.' My state of mind started to spiral downwards each day. The negative voices almost lead me to give up trying. My head was telling me to stick with the job I knew even though it was not lighting my fire anymore, but my heart was burning for creativity and once again, that hidden voice came back telling me that I had to carry on.

Some days Facebook would be the only place I'd see people, perhaps looking back now I was lonelier than I knew and one morning, I caught a live by a lady talking about positivity and mindset. She was talking about positivity, using positive language, and using gratitude. It was like someone had turned on a spotlight, like she was talking to me. I realised that I had literally been talking myself down, so I had to build myself back up.

I began to learn about setting goals, manifesting, and visualising what I wanted. Staying in that new positive place I found that I had to remove lots of negativity, so I stopped watching the news, avoided certain people, certain influences, and situations. I slowly started to believe in me, and people were seeing my business because I believed in it. Then people who ran the Facebook communities I was in started ordering from little old me. It blew my mind. They believed in me.

As all these new layers of positivity were building

up, I then learned all about vision boards another star in my positive new universe. I could actually see the things I wanted using pictures and words; I knew this new positive language was my new medicine and over the months more spiritual elements came into my world. I was attracting them: crystals, journaling, being introduced to new circles of women who understood me. Often hearing the terms, 'find your tribe' and 'find the right circle for you' and finally I had. I found them because they were being brought into my world. I was attracting them, each one supported me in a different way, showing me, I was strong, resilient, and courageous.

Then on 21st December 2022, our world was turned upside down, on my way back home surrounded by traffic everywhere due to three local accidents, I received a phone call from my sister. I instinctively knew what she was going to say. It was my husband in one of those accidents and that there were police at my house, ready to take me to the hospital.

As the policeman took me to the hospital, I was expecting the worst, but they couldn't tell me anything as the police radio system has crashed. In the shock I could feel I was sinking deeper, sounds around me started to be muffled, we arrived before the ambulance. He had been rescued by the air ambulance crew but was coming in by land ambulance. He was alive but I was told that the next few hours would be critical. The police and doctor both told me that an accident so bad doesn't normally see any survivors.

Being allowed to see him was very strange as there was a team of doctors around him, everything sounded so alien. He was able to speak to me and told me to go home to be with our daughter, which I did. In the morning, I was told that he was virtually broken from shoulder to toe. I knew I had to be strong to get us through this and to bring our little family through this.

At that point I could have quite easily given up on my newfound positive way of life as some anger started creeping back in. At that point I couldn't see how there could be anything positive about that? Why did this happen? I could have fallen into that old script but that self-talk would have been so damming.

Luckily something kept saying in my head, 'You must keep going. You must be strong. You must carry on!'

That night I went straight back to my gratitude diary, asking to keep him alive, to heal all those broken bones, to mend all those internal injuries. I wrote gratitude for the crews that helped him, firefighters, and the nurse first on the scene, air ambulance doctors.

Every day I wrote my gratitude list, morning, and night.

I was encouraged by the ICU staff to keep a diary of how each day was, describing the days, procedures he'd had done, so when the sedation was lifted, I could fill any gaps for him. Looking back, I think it helped me more to get my feelings out each day. I wrote it like a letter, remembering to include any funny items as sense of humour had always been a key part in our relationship.

As the days passed, he got stronger and as the surgeons started to rebuild his bones, he started to come around, although at times in terrible pain. This was where I had to be even stronger as we still didn't know what we were looking at in the long term and especially if he would walk again. We had to lip read whilst the tracheotomy was still in, lip reading was both frustrating especially when he was confused by the amounts of medication and the ICU delirium.

I had family and good friends around me daily, and other friends messaging daily but I know now that it was my own belief and strength that got me through each day. Being positive, believing there was a better life out there for us, and that sense of humour I mentioned kept us going. I'm so glad I took to my diary with the funny moments as those are what we need to remember.

As the weeks went on, he got stronger and at the time of writing he still has a way to go but is walking, talking, and occasionally still driving me mad but more importantly still making me laugh.

Seeing life change in the blink of an eye really makes you see things differently. After such a sharp change to our family dynamics it made me think we can't just 'carry on' this time something must change. As I had to be home more to care for Rob it opened time to start being more creative with my business, sharing my passion for creativity with others, it was my therapy.

My mission is to show as many people as possible that being creative can really help to ease the strain, it's relaxing, it's freeing, it can be a release. So, as well as using gratitude and positivity grab a piece of paper and doodle, grab some colouring books and pens and what I always say is don't worry about what you create just enjoy the process. It's time for quiet and time to switch off. Add in your new positive words and gratitude in your doodles, even if things feel beyond hope be grateful for the little things believe and feel every single one you write. I promise it will make a difference.

ABOUT THE AUTHOR

CLARE GOULD-SMITH

Clare, wife and mum of one daughter is happiest at home with her family and her crafting supplies. She also loves being outside and by the sea.

Forever a creative, her business fills all the dreams she had growing up and in adult life, to be creative each day, making and creating personalised gifts, to more recently sharing her passion with crafty circles, showing ladies how to relax with creativity. Showing them that being creative isn't always about having a finished masterpiece but enjoying the process.

Clare has a degree in Art and more recently qualifications in Art therapy, Clare runs monthly local and online Crafty Circles.

You can reach Clare at:

www.facebook.com/profile.php?id=100084124144853

NOT ALL RAINBOWS AND FAIRY DUST

By Sara Hughes

I woke up with tears pouring down my face. I was twenty-three years old and felt like I had failed my babies, myself, and my family who I should have listened to seven years before. If I had listened, then I wouldn't have been laying there with bruised ribs flinching with fear at my child's hug and innocently touching my neck due to the violence I had suffered.

Every day I heard the words from my family repeated in my mind, "I TOLD YOU SO," and would wake up shaking myself out of that dream, which was my living nightmare. The horror of my dream replaced by the noise of my six-month-old boy crying for a bottle and my two and four-year-old playing and giggling.

I felt so scared for my girls and what they witnessed, and worried about how it would impact them in the future. The look of my girl's faces will haunt me forever. The guilt of them seeing it when I should have protected them sooner, but I didn't as I didn't have the strength until that final day, I snapped. I called the police before he broke in and broke my phone. He would have made me into a worthless, petrified girl like he always did.

For seven years my life was torture, windows being smashed, banks rinsed for dealers' debt. To get away I used to flee to my mums in Rhyl for weeks to try and protect us.

Social services finally placed us in a safe house in Stockport where I didn't know anybody. I learned to manage being a young single mum to three babies not knowing where the next meal was coming from. I arranged meetings with solicitors to get a divorce from a monster I called a husband that I had been married to for eighteen months.

After three months of living in a safe house I was finally given a home of my own for me and my babies, finally a fresh start for us which I then went onto buy, this was a huge vision of mine. When we went to court, I was hopeful that through the court process I would come away with a sense of justice, but I walked away feeling like I failed again as I wasn't able to get this man the punishment, he deserved for what he done to me and my babies. He walked away with a fine and two-year suspended sentence. My confidence was knocked again, and the feeling of failure would just not leave my side.

It took me a few years to start to feel like I belonged where I was living, I had great neighbours and amazing friends. I then got a job and getting that call to say I got the job was like a dream. It was a tough couple of weeks sorting childcare and getting into a routine, but I did it. Little old me started getting some confidence back. It took me a few years to feel like I was not just a mum but Sara too.

In 2015 I was presented with an opportunity to do something for me on my own terms as a side hustle. I joined a great online community and was making something of myself. I managed to save up and took my babies on their first family holiday to Tunisia. I was starting to live the life I dreamed of taking the kids away, days out life was amazing.

My feeling of freedom didn't last long as he came back on the scene, and everything came crashing down around me. It was like he was back for revenge. My boy had an accident and the hospital called social services and that was it, all those feelings from that twenty-three-year-old me came back and came back one hundred times worse. I lost a court battle and lost my children to the monster I had worked so hard on protecting them from. It left me feeling so hurt, like a failure and angry. I became more lost than ever before as this time I didn't have my children by my side to pick me up. I completely lost myself. I used to lock myself away, not eat and not socialise. I didn't recognise myself I was just a body without a soul; a black hole, existing not living.

It was two years of pure hell, each time I handed the kids back a piece of me, went with them, each weekend was like my worst nightmare. But then I had to kick myself each time and tell myself as easy as it would been to walk away, I was not going to be that person. I knew that those kids needed their mama no matter what.

October 2017 came, I met a man online and instantly connected. He made me feel so safe and loved, things moved quickly by December 2018 I moved in with him and his daughter and I put my house on the market as to me it was a shell not a home it was a place to sleep that was all. It wasn't my kids' home; it wasn't my home.

The following year we decided to get a new house as the two-bed flat was not big enough for two adults and five kids, so we got a three-bed private house. Life was picking up; my main job was going well, and my side biz was doing okay and paid for the extras we wanted so it served its purpose. The day we were moving I got a call from the kids' dad, and I just cried down the phone as he told me he was handing the kids back to me. I completely broke down with relief and excitement. I felt paralysed and numb. I just sobbed when my babies were coming home.

It was the most amazing feeling picking my kids up in August 2018 to bring them back home for good to where they belonged. Life was a bit of a roller coaster having two families come together. It wasn't always rainbows and fairy dust, it was tough. Then lockdown happened and wow that brought its challenges.

Me and my partner were both furloughed and having five kids constantly at home was crazy and stressful. I almost hit breaking point and had to go to my mum's for a few days to clear my head or my relationship would have been over as I was struggling so much. I sat on Facebook and saw a post from a friend about her crystal order she received, and I was so drawn to them I had to ask her where she got them from as we weren't allowed out to shop. She gave me the details of the group the lady ran and then that was it, I was absolutely hooked on crystals. I started to learn about them and how best to use them.

As time went by, I started to really struggle with my side biz. I was having coaching sessions with the most amazing lady Lisa, the host of this book. I just couldn't put my finger on what the issue was, I had all these sessions but was not moving forward. Something was holding me back massively. Then in May 2023 we had a face-to-face session, Lisa helped me dig through some traumas that I had not realised were holding me back. I would never tell my partner I was doing something; I would always seek permission and if I did anything I would always feel like I had to overcompensate for me not being around and felt guilty leaving my children with him. Lisa said I should go to Womanifest with her and just tell my partner I was going as she knew I was making every excuse up I could not to go even though deep down I had to be there, I wanted to be there. So that night I went home, and I just said to my partner, "In July I am going to a wellbeing festival," his response made me cry, he just simply went, "Okay that's fine." I felt sick even telling him I was going but afterwards the feeling was incredible that I didn't seek permission it was like a huge weight had just lifted. I felt like a bit of the feisty confident Sara was popping back through. I went to the festival and never felt so alive as I did that weekend, it opened my eyes so much about me and what I wanted from life.

In August 2023 I was having another session with Lisa, and she simply asked me what I wanted to talk about, and my response was, "I don't want to do it anymore," I had realised that my business was not aligned anymore and so on 26th August 2023 *The Crystal Fairy Godmother* was born. I have never felt so aligned to anything than I have since starting my own business with crystals helping adults and children to find joy within crystals so they can live a happy and empowering life like I now do.

I have finally turned my life around and it's going in the right direction. I have the most amazing ladies around me who support me not just in business but in life also, I owe my life to these ladies. They helped me to find not the old Sara but the new Sara that I needed to become.

I have become my own Fairy Godmother sprinkling my own fairy dust when it's needed to live the life I choose and not the life someone maps out for me. I am brave, I am strong, I am confident, and I am ME. If you are currently going through some tough times just remember there is always a rainbow after the storm and you can achieve everything you deserve, do not give up!

ABOUT THE AUTHOR

SARA HUGHES

The Crystal Fairy Godmother, Sara is a dedicated mother of three and a loving step mum of two. In her role as The Crystal Fairy Godmother, she focuses on supporting women and children, helping them discover joy and empowerment using crystals.

Despite facing significant trauma, Sara has demonstrated remarkable resilience, emerging stronger and inspiring those around her. With several years of experience in the property sector, she also manages her own business, where she brings joy and positivity into people's lives through her work with crystals.

Sara is easily recognised by her love for the colour yellow and her reliance on coffee to get through her busy days.

Despite the rollercoaster of life, she continues to show up, sprinkling her unique brand of Fairy magic wherever she goes.

You can reach Sara at:

www.facebook.com/groups/1385033668895092

FINDING LIGHT IN THE SHADOWS

By Emma Ellis

On March 13th, 2023, our world changed forever when my beautiful girl, Luna, was diagnosed with Pallister-Killian syndrome. This rare chromosomal disorder, with fewer than five hundred cases documented worldwide, became a central part of our lives. The diagnosis was a shock, throwing us into a world of medical jargon and uncertainty.

Pallister-Killian syndrome is often confused with Down syndrome due to similar physical characteristics. Luna's tongue sticks out, her eyes are wide apart, and they have a unique almond shape. People would often ask if Luna had Down syndrome, and I would say I believe so, thinking that was the case. But when the doctors explained that her condition was Pallister-Killian syndrome I was left shocked.

The day of the diagnosis is stuck in my memory. I was sitting in the hospital side-room feeling so sick with worry and like I couldn't breathe as the words, "Pallister-Killian syndrome," sank in. I started shaking my head and kept saying, "No this can't be right." I had braced myself for a Down syndrome diagnosis, but this rare condition, something even the doctors knew little about, was terrifying. I kept thinking to myself if the doctors don't understand it fully, how on earth are we going to cope and help Luna? I couldn't stop crying, overwhelmed by fears for Luna's future. Would she ever walk or talk? What kind of life would she have?

Learning that Pallister-Killian syndrome occurs randomly, with no known cause, was another blow. A roll of the genetic dice, this random mutation during the formation of the egg meant there was no way to predict or prevent it. Even though I knew all this I still blamed myself and kept thinking back over the pregnancy on what if and hoping to find an answer as to why it happened to my beautiful little girl. I hated life for so long and all I wanted to do was curl up on the bed with her and not get out. I kept hugging her so tight and cried for weeks on end. I found myself searching the internet for information, desperately trying to make sense of it all. But all I found were more questions and very few answers. Each new piece of information led to more uncertainty, leaving me feeling more lost than before but no matter what challenges lay ahead, I knew I would be there to support her.

Despite the fear and uncertainty, one thing remains constant: my love for Luna. She is my girl, and I love her with all my heart. Every small progress she has made has been such an amazing feeling inside. Even something as small as her first smile, when she first rolled over onto her side and all the little things we take for granted, each moment is a victory and makes me get so excited. It just shows us that she is determined herself to do this through her strength and resilience. Every milestone, no matter how small, fills my heart with hope and reminds me of her incredible spirit.

Shortly after the diagnosis, Luna caught respiratory syncytial virus (RSV), a common virus that can be particularly dangerous for infants or anyone with a genetic disorder. Luna's condition rapidly deteriorated, and we found ourselves in the hospital's high dependency unit (HDU). Seeing her hooked up to machines, fighting to breathe, was one of the scariest experiences of my life. The beeping of monitors, the smell of the hospital, and the constant influx of doctors and nurses created an atmosphere of relentless anxiety. Sitting in the HDU room just staring at blank white walls and constantly hearing beeps while having no one there to support me was so hard as I knew I had to be strong for her, but all I could do was cry and beg her to pull through. Watching her tiny chest rise and fall with such effort was a painful reminder of her fragility.

There were moments when the fear was overwhelming. I worried that I wouldn't be able to care for a child with such complex needs. The future seemed daunting, filled with challenges I didn't know if I could face. But deep down, I believed that the universe wouldn't have given me this amazing, sweet girl if it didn't think I could handle it. Somehow, someway, I would find the strength to support her. Each day was a test of my strength, pushing me to be stronger and more resilient than I ever thought possible.

Luna's diagnosis and illness forced me to confront my own fears and doubts. There were days when I felt strong, ready to take on the world for her but there were also days when all I wanted to do was hide away and cry. It was during these dark moments that Luna's light shone the brightest. Her innocent joy, her pure happiness, reminded me that life is filled with moments of beauty and grace, even in the middle of all that was going on. Her smile gave me hope, guiding me through the darkest times and giving me the courage to face another day.

Inspired by Luna's resilience, I began to seek out ways to find my own strength. I researched tirelessly on the internet and joined Facebook communities of other parents with children who had Pallister-Killian syndrome. These communities became my lifeline, offering support, advice, and a sense of belonging. I found comfort in knowing that I wasn't alone, that there were others who understood my struggles and fears. Reading the stories of other parents who faced similar challenges was a sign of hope, guiding me through the darkest times. These connections were not just a source of information but a source of emotional support, helping me navigate this complex journey.

One of the most powerful tools I discovered was the practice of gratitude. Each day, I started to write down three things that I was grateful for. This simple practice helped me shift my focus from what was lacking in my life to the abundance that was already there. It wasn't always easy, but with each passing day, I began to see the world in a different light. On particularly tough days, finding even the smallest things to be grateful for became a lifeline, pulling me back from the brink of despair. Whether it was the warmth of the sun on my face or a kind word from a friend, these moments of gratitude became the anchors that kept me grounded.

Another crucial aspect of my journey was learning to be kinder to myself. I realised that self-compassion was essential for my growth. I started to treat myself with the same kindness and understanding that I showed to others. This shift in perspective allowed me to embrace my imperfections and see them as part of my unique journey. I learned to forgive myself for the moments of doubt and fear, understanding that they were a natural part of this challenging journey. Each day, I reminded myself that it was okay to struggle, and that strength comes from acknowledging and facing those struggles head-on.

Throughout this process, I discovered the power of community. Surrounding myself with positive, supportive people made a significant difference. Their encouragement and understanding helped me stay motivated and inspired. Together, we celebrated the small wins and supported each other through the tough times. I found solace in knowing that I wasn't alone, that there were others who understood my struggles and fears. These connections were not just a source of support, but a source of strength, reminding me that together, we could overcome any obstacle. Their shared experiences and collective wisdom provided me with the tools I needed to navigate this journey with hope and resilience.

Today, I am a different person. I am inspired and filled with a sense of purpose. Luna, now two years old, continues to be my guiding light, showing me the beauty of resilience and the power of love. My journey has taught me that positive change is possible, even in the face of adversity. Her joy and determination have become my strength, driving me to be the best mother I can be. Every day, I am grateful for the lessons she teaches me, the resilience she embodies, and the love she radiates. Luna's spirit has not only transformed my life but has also touched the lives of everyone around her.

Remember, the road to positive change is not always easy, but it is worth it. Embrace the journey, celebrate your progress, and never lose sight of the incredible power you hold within you. You have the ability to inspire, to motivate, and to create a life filled with joy and purpose. Luna has taught me that, and I hope my story can inspire you to find your own light. Let Luna's story be a reminder that even in the face of adversity, there is always hope and the potential for profound growth.

As we move forward, I hold onto the belief that together, Luna and our family can face anything.

Her spirit shines so brightly, it lights up even our darkest moments. And as she grows, I know she will continue to teach me and everyone around her the true meaning of strength, love, and resilience. Each new milestone, each new challenge overcome, is a testament to her spirit and our bond as a family. Our journey is a testament to the power of love and the unbreakable bond between a mother and her child.

If there is one message, I want to leave you with, it is this: no matter where you are right now, know that you have the strength within you to create the life you desire. Take that first step, no matter how small, and trust that the universe will guide you. Surround yourself with positivity, practise gratitude, and be kind to yourself. Your journey is unique, and every step you take is a testament to your strength and courage. Believe in yourself and the power of your journey, for it is through these challenges that you will find your true strength and purpose.

This journey with Luna has not been easy, but it has been filled with lots of moments of growth and love. I am grateful for every smile, every challenge, and every victory, no matter how small. Luna is my beautiful girlie, my moon baby, and I will cherish and support her, no matter what the future holds. The journey ahead may be uncertain, but with love and determination, we will face it together. Each step forward is a step towards a brighter future, filled with love, hope, and endless possibilities.

ABOUT THE AUTHOR

EMMA ELLIS

Emma is a dedicated mother of four girls, with her youngest being diagnosed with Pallister-Killian syndrome, a rare genetic disorder. Balancing her full-time role as an admin assistant, Emma also thrives in her network marketing and digital marketing businesses, aspiring to transition them into her primary career.

Her achievements include double promotions in network marketing and completing the Oracle medicine course, paving the way for her Oracle card readings. Passionate about spirituality, Emma is keen on learning spiritual healing techniques to launch a spiritual healing business.

Her core value of helping others drives her mission to support stay-at-home mums through her ventures. Emma is committed to making a positive impact, whether through her healing practices or by empowering others to achieve financial independence and spend more time with their families.

You can reach Emma at:

https://www.facebook.com/share/n1s17JzhLhwjh3Nv/

THE JOURNEY TO REAL LOVE

By Louise Anne

I stood in the hallway with my sisters sobbing uncontrollably next to me. My father, the reason for their emotional distress, was still yelling at them. I was only about fourteen and as everything played out, I felt like a spectator. His voice was muffled through the blood pumping through my ears, my vision was blurry and even if I wanted to move - my body was no longer in my control. He had always been quite an angry man, but this was a whole new level. What we later discovered was that this event was his last hoorah. His big crescendo before leaving our lives forever.

My father was emotionally abusive and had spent years triangulating my sisters and me. The old 'divide and conquer' and this event was no different. He told my sisters that the only daughter he wanted a relationship with - was me. My world crumbled. I had spent my entire childhood begging to be wanted and loved by my dad and now what I yearned for was being weaponised against my sisters. The fall out at that time was more than I could cope with. It was the straw that broke the camel's back. Something in me snapped. I developed an eating disorder and suffered from anxiety and depression. I started to self-harm and became suicidal. I was about fifteen when I tried to take my own life.

The truth was that I was trauma bonded to my father. Years of love bombing, gaslighting and criticism had left their scars.

I was like an addict. When he would love bomb, he would shower me with praise and attention. I felt euphoric. But just like any drug, the high would not last and he would quickly change and start to criticise me. The stress of not knowing what would set off this change caused me to be constantly living on eggshells. Never knowing what reaction my actions would receive.

The problem was that I longed for that high. The bliss I felt when he would be the father I longed for, and I finally felt that maybe he loved me.

When my father was no longer giving me those brief moments of feeling loved, it was like going cold turkey when I wasn't ready to quit. I craved to feel that way again.

When I was seventeen, I met a man, he was obsessed with me. When we first started dating, we saw each other nearly every day. When we didn't, he would call and talk to me for hours on the phone. It felt so right because it felt so familiar. We were engaged when I was eighteen. Then things turned, I started to struggle with my mental health when I was nineteen, he made me promise to not, 'do anything stupid.' I made a promise to him that I would not take my own life. He was my saviour and took control of my life. I wasn't allowed male friends, I stopped going out, I even changed what I wore to his preference. It's strange how cycles continue until the lesson is learned.

This time though it was my daughters crying and my husband yelling at me, the man that I had once believed had saved me. It was ten years after my father left and I guess from the outside it looked like I had done rather well. I was married, had two incredible and healthy daughters, owned a semi-detached house, and had a career in finance.

But there I was again. His voice was muffled through the blood pumping through my ears, my vision was blurry, and I was unable to move. I had just told him that I was filing for divorce, and he was angry. Six months prior to this conversation I had found out that he had been having an affair with a woman at work. Our youngest had just turned one and I desperately wanted my daughters to have stability. So, for six months I had been working on the marriage. I say 'I' because he never did. I told him multiple times a week that our marriage wasn't going to survive with them working together. Despite giving him time and trying to encourage him, he refused to look for another job. After six months I realised that he didn't want to save the marriage. He didn't love me.

He didn't love me enough to stay faithful, and he didn't love me enough to walk away from her.

Once again, the dark void of depression took hold. My ex had looked me in the eye and told me that he wasn't going to be the reason I didn't die. He told me that he released me from my promise. The promise I made not to end my life, and he 'released' me from it when I needed it the most. How could a man that once told me he loved me do this to me?

Fortunately, I was under the care of the most amazing doctor. He told me to make a promise to someone 'better.' If that's what I needed to do - then to do it.

I sat on the floor of my daughter's bedroom while they slept, and I made a promise to my precious daughters. My three-year-old and eighteen-month-old, I promised them that I would survive for them.

I wish that had been the hardest part. But it wasn't. His affair was the key to my gilded cage. The following year emotional abuse became illegal in the UK, and I finally understood what I had actually been recovering from. Things started to make sense about the treatment I had normalised because of what I had experienced as a child. The fear, the anxiety, and the control. It was how my dad had been, and it was the only form of 'love' I had ever known from a male. It was what I believed relationships to be.

In the space of a year, my life had fallen apart. I filed for divorce, I was made redundant from my job, I became homeless, and I was a single mum to two daughters. But life never throws you overboard without giving you a lifeline.

I found mine in a rock pub on a night out. My sister and I were on a night out while the girls were with their dad. I went out whenever the girls were with him, the house was too empty without them. The silence hurt.

On one of these nights out there were a group that kept bumping into us, until a stranger came and stood in the way. He had his back towards us and stood guard. After that I nicknamed him the bodyguard. It was another couple of weeks before I saw him again and finally could say thank you. Dave and I became friends and when I needed a night out, he was there. I even became his wingman and tried to help him with the ladies.

On the following Valentine's Day, we went out together as friends and after a three-course meal and listening to London symphony orchestra, we ended the night as boyfriend and girlfriend.

Months later when the sale finally went through on the marital house, it was him that gave me somewhere to stay while the girls moved in with their father. He was the one that helped me find somewhere to live and supported me while I started a new job. He made sure the girls and I had food in the fridge and treats in the cupboard when I was struggling to pay for childcare so I could work fulltime.

We started dating and told the girls. Dave continued to rent his own place and the girls asked for months (literally) when Dave was going to move in. I was scared, but I didn't want my past to dictate the future of my life.

I decided that I was worthy of love and happiness and so I was going to allow it into my life.

I changed the way I spoke to myself; I began journaling, EFT and meditation. I healed my limiting beliefs and began taking care of my well-being.

I didn't want to spend the rest of my life as a victim of my past, and I didn't want that for my daughters either. I realised that it was my responsibility to live the life I was telling my daughters was possible. They deserved to know what a healthy and loving relationship looked like, and so did I. They deserved to know that men could be kind, good and loving. That fear and anxiety weren't normal feelings to have in your home. They deserved to experience the childhood I had longed for.

We moved in together and the following year bought a house. One that was big enough for us to have more children and we were blessed with two more daughters.

My eldest has cut contact with her biological father due to his treatment of her. She put boundaries in place and when he ignored them and dismissed her - she knew that she deserved better. She understood more at thirteen than I did in my thirties.

I now teach others the tools and techniques that I have learned using the *Abused to Empowered® Framework*. Transforming my life didn't happen in the sessions I attended with professionals but in the day-to-day actions I took. The girls and I all get to experience the beauty of a loving and safe home. The beauty of a kind and supportive partner and the possibilities of a life lived with purpose.

All because I chose to heal my past, and free my future.

ABOUT THE AUTHOR

LOUISE ANNE

Louise is an award-winning Female Empowerment Coach, NLP Master Practitioner, EFT Practitioner and Keynote speaker. She is a mum of four daughters with a passion for the education and empowerment of those that have experienced abuse and toxic relationships. 2013 Louise discovered her husband was having an affair. When his behaviour towards her got worse she filed for divorce. In the months that followed she was made redundant from her job, became homeless and was on medication for her deteriorating mental health. When emotional abuse became illegal in the UK in 2015 she finally started to understand what she had been recovering from. She also saw the parallels with the treatment she had witnessed from her own father growing up. Knowing that she wasn't going to allow her daughters to normalise abuse the way she had, Louise went on a mission to learn all she could about healing her mental health. She wanted to learn things that she could teach her daughters. Tools and techniques that could be normalised in day-to-day life. Everything she learned she put into the Abused to Empowered® Framework, an online self-study course teaching practical changes to transform and heal. Now Louise is in a loving and secure relationship, owns her own 5 bed house and runs a successful coaching business as well as travelling the country sharing her story on stage. "Heal your past to free your future"

You can reach Louise at:

www.louise-anne.co.uk

GRATITUDE SAVED ME

By Lisa Williams

I sat in disbelief with what I had just heard, my eyes filled with tears and everything I knew had gone in a blink of an eye. My body filled with fear, panic of what all this meant for me and my unborn child. The moments which followed were a blur, I couldn't grasp what was being said as the news sunk in that, "All vulnerable and pregnant women were to stay at home." Being pregnant was a dream come true after experiencing several miscarriages which began in 2016 and finally carrying my rainbow baby, I envisioned being happy, free, and living my dream. Being stuck at home was not part of that plan.

Schools were closed, I wasn't allowed out and my whole world was crushed. At the time I worked doing payroll for a local accountancy firm. I had some 'side hustles' but nothing that came close to paying my bills. As I wasn't allowed to go into the office, they brought the office to me, my living room was full of files and paperwork; it was overwhelming. My mindset plummeted to an all-time low, I struggled to keep up with the home schooling and having my office at home there was just no escape, everything was cluttered, and I felt like I couldn't breathe. After spending a few weeks crying every day I knew I couldn't carry on until my maternity kicked in, so I ended up going off sick, something I had never done before.

My husband was classed as a key worker due to the manufacturing industry he worked in and so every day when he left for work my stomach would do somersaults, I would sit crying with the news in the background trying to understand what was happening. Prior to lockdown my husband would get the bus to work as we only had one car in the house, so to reduce any risk of public places he started taking my car. In less than twenty-four hours from that first announcement I had lost going out, lost going to work and lost my car. My independence had been stripped! As an independent woman I felt lost and inside I felt numb with fear.

The first time I went out of my house in a car was to my hospital appointment, a few days prior to the 'stay home' announcement I had been diagnosed with gestational diabetes, which meant more regular check-ups, I was already under a consultant due to my recurrent miscarriages, so this meant more hospital trips. I now had to go on my own, due to restrictions. This gave me anxiety and having experienced trauma around my miscarriages any appointment triggered this PTSD (post-traumatic stress disorder). My body would fill with fear, so going alone was even worse, it kept me awake at night worrying, it made me feel sick for days prior. Being pregnant after miscarriages is hard enough, never mind this added worry of COVID without your support network by your side holding your hand was soul destroying and scary.

I pulled up at the hospital at the end of March 2020, bearing in mind I had not been anywhere in a few weeks other than a walk around my block, my eyes filled with tears. I looked around me and saw several ambulances and the paramedics full of protective clothing, with gas mask type masks on. I felt like I had just walked into a sci-fi film. I sat and cried for at least five minutes, I felt motionless, my stomach churning with a sickly feeling of anxiety rippling through me.

Three weeks into staying at home I began my sick leave which eventually converted into maternity leave. Every day I eagerly waited for updates and answers on the news, but nothing came. Each day I worried about leaving the house to protect my unborn child, but I pushed myself to enjoy a daily walk. Each evening when hubby got home I had him strip at the door and go straight in the shower, so he didn't pass anything onto us, now looking back it feels silly, but we were living in a crazy world right? Every day I felt anxious and confused.

One of my biggest challenges was the home-schooling; this was most definitely one of the hardest things I have ever done but the silver lining was that I did start to enjoy the slower pace of life. I enjoyed the walks with my seven-year-old daughter. We began to venture a little further on our walks and often went to a bench on the seafront. I found a sense of calm there. Alysa would run free and burn all her energy on the grass banks and I just sat in stillness embracing the views, this was where I really felt grateful.

As time went on, I began to grip to those happier moments of walks, crafts, nature and embrace them. I began writing a gratitude journal, I started writing down ten things I was grateful for each morning, I made a conscious effort to start to embrace each beautiful moment we had, I focused on being healthy in my pregnancy and slowly my mindset shifted.

As my mindset began to shift, I felt a new light inside me, I felt optimistic again. Prior to lockdown I had already been working on my mindset for around three years, I had some tools inside me which I could dig out and use. Once I finally turned that corner, I began to implement those tools, I started to change my negative thinking into positive, I began to change how I spoke about things. The biggest thing is I STOPPED watching the news and I put myself and my family inside my positive bubble. In this newfound mindset shift I began working on my new business, something which had been an idea some months prior to lockdown but I had not implemented anything due to focusing on my pregnancy. I found that I had time on my hands, and I used that time to take action!

When I was amid the anxiety and fears of what was happening in life, my journal became my best friend. Not only did I write my daily gratitude I began using my journal to uncover some of my past traumas. I began exploring my money mindset, my triggers and other blocks which held me back, it was a time of healing my inner self at a time the world was all hurting. I began to show up and become visible online sharing my positive mindset, I was stepping into my purpose as the 'Vision Board Queen,' which is exactly why I have put together this collaboration book. To give the reader a bank of motivational and inspirational tools to help them on their life's journey.

One of my biggest lessons from this journey was to protect myself, sometimes outside sources like media, work, people can influence our feelings, this was exactly what happened during this period to me. This can happen anytime in life, but you do have a choice to accept those feelings, or you can choose to create your own story. I chose to create my own story and turn those negative feelings around with the help of my daily gratitude. My challenge for you is to embrace those magical moments of each day and choose to live in a place of gratitude each day.

Working on myself is still a huge part of my daily life, even though I now have a stronger mindset I still work on me every day. My daily routine is a crucial element of my morning, without this I would not be writing this today in a position of strength. This routine consists of gratitude journaling, journaling around my blocks, connecting with crystals, oracle cards and reading self-help books. I also spend a few minutes each morning connecting with my vision board, making sure that the actions I take that day are a step closer to the dreams and desires on that board. Yes, this can sometimes be tricky with two girls around me each morning, but I have made this non-negotiable. If I don't work on me then my girls do not get the best version of me.

The 'Vision Board Queen' people see today, definitely was not the same person who placed that crown on her head in April 2020. I have grown so much as a person and as an entrepreneur. I love to help and support other women giving them that light to shine as they step into their future version of themselves.

ABOUT THE AUTHOR

LISA WILLIAMS

Lisa Williams, known as the Vision Board Queen, is a trained vision board coach dedicated to helping business women design the blueprints for their dream life and achieving the freedom they desire. Lisa has achieved several of her own visionary dreams, including her dream wedding and the birth of her beautiful rainbow baby. Passionate about vision boards and the law of attraction, Lisa transformed her life from being a 'Negative Nelly' to a beacon of positivity by changing her mindset.

As a best-selling author, podcast host, and practitioner of NLP and journaling therapy, Lisa works with businesswomen both online and offline to help them achieve their dreams. She offers support through her sisterhood community, group coaching, one-on-one coaching, and workshops.

Additionally, Lisa organises visionary and strategy days that bring women together to focus on their aspirations. Her mission is to empower others to live the life they desire.

Lisa's journey began in 2016 when she experienced her first miscarriage while trying for her second child, followed by another loss in early 2017. These heart-breaking events pushed her into a dark place, but she found solace and direction in network marketing. This path sparked her personal growth journey and initiated her healing process. Despite the challenges, Lisa committed to incorporating personal growth into her daily routine—a practice she continues to this day and teaches to her clients.

Lisa is a proud mother of two girls and remains dedicated to helping others turn their dreams into reality through the power of vision boards and a positive mindset.

You can reach Lisa at:

www.lisawilliams-lmg.co.uk/contact

THE RAINBOW AFTER THE STORM

By Hannah Louise Barker

During lockdown I lost myself and I felt alone. I was on maternity leave with my newborn son and so I found being isolated and not able to see my family so hard. Not only did I not have their support, but they missed out on bonding with their new grandson. When lockdown was announced I felt so scared of the uncertainty that came with it, I could feel myself losing my identity. I needed something to keep me occupied in lockdown, especially not knowing how long we would be isolated for. I needed to find the spark within me again because I felt I'd lost it I wanted to find myself again but didn't know how to find my spark.

I was looking for connection with people especially when I discovered network marketing. There I began to look for something to help how I was feeling. I knew I deserved more and was made for more; I needed the motivation to be able to get the motion moving. I noticed how much I'd been stuck in my own head with negativity spiralling around, the feelings of feeling unworthy and the lack of confidence I've always been fearful of change and lockdown had tested my anxiety more than usual with the feeling of the unknown of what was going to happen. I had a light bulb moment where I knew I wanted to change the feelings I had, I wanted to create change and be the best version of me I could be.

I began to seek community with networking online via Facebook groups and zooms, making friends online, I even managed to find the love for my own self-care by being part of the Body Shop at Home. I started to feel my spark returning I had the determination and the drive to achieve something and to feel fulfilled. I listened to trainings about self-development and altering my mindset I discovered the power of journaling and I started to learn about the power of brain dumping all the negative thoughts out of my head onto paper which changed my perspective on how the things I wrote down felt worse in my head than when I put pen to paper. I began to show myself compassion, self-love, and awareness of how I was feeling. I was able to show strength, I knew change needed to happen because I no longer wanted to keep being in the cycle of negativity. I had high hopes for myself and that I deserved more, but I knew that work on myself needed to happen.

I looked further into myself development journey this helped me to find the motivation for changes to occur and it allowed me to create new habits and transformation to break the cycle of negativity that I was in. I started to listen to motivational podcasts and books on audible to help me. The one book which changed my negativity was 'Good Life, Good Vibes' by Vex King. When I started listening to his book, I felt the same as he was feeling at the beginning of the book. I was feeling lost, deflated, unmotivated and uninspired and so I started to input small habits to help me. I had the extended time to create memories with my family and even though we were in lockdown it made me appreciate the things I'd once taken for granted such as connection with other people. Through reading this book I started to create small changes and being able to shift how I was feeling even though I had a lot of work to do it was a starting point for me.

Fast forward to 2022 I continued to create habits through tools I'd learned from self-development the habits I created were through journaling, mediation, brain dumping all my thoughts of negativity onto paper to clear space in my head. I began to change my circumstances using affirmations. I was able to challenge and reframe my negative feelings and turn them into affirmations to support me. I discovered the power of mindful breathing to help me with my anxiety.

I started to break the negative cycle which came from being around negative people and I started to find the positives by having a consistent practice of everything that was happening for me. I found an awakening through self-development, affirmations, meditations, and mindful breathing. I was working on myself finding things that would light me up such as pole dancing which is something that has helped me feel confident and given me self-belief that I can achieve anything I set my mind to. I found joy and passion within pole dancing, and I know how much it helped me in my dark times.

I attended in person events to get inspiration; I attended an event where I shared my story to help empower others and to create the impact which pushed me out of my comfort zone and to allow me to step into my growth zone. I did find it difficult to keep on track with the motivation and to get started with doing tasks. I knew I could push through and find my inspiration and self-belief.

I didn't want to feel unmotivated anymore and I wanted my children to see me as a good role model to look up to. I wanted to show them that with adversity and any setbacks you have to get back up again to be able to find ways to handle the challenges with courage, confidence and rebuild yourself without having the feeling of disempowerment but to come from a place of power. I found myself really challenged in January 2023 suffering a baby loss made me question myself for things not always going my way. I wanted to change, and I had the tools to help me.

When I began my journey with finding motivation again after my miscarriage loss my mindset was affected with low moods and demotivation. This miscarriage hit me the hardest and my emotions were all over the place. I knew that how I was feeling was normal and my emotions were completely valid as there's no right or wrong way to express your emotions when dealing with grief because it was all part of the process of coming to terms with it. I decided to come away from social media so I could start to rebuild myself again I gave myself permission to grieve for my baby for as long as I needed. I used my journal to help me write my feelings down. Journaling helped me to express myself freely so I could begin my grieving process having suffered two previous miscarriages before.

When I arrived at the hospital, I was given the bad news that my pregnancy would end and a torrent of emotions flooded through me from anger, sadness, helpless, confused, and annoyed. I had a meeting to find out what had caused this to happen which was identified as the illness CMV when I had the time for grieving, I had to tell my children the news I knew I had to be strong telling them which I did through a book given to us.

I grieved for as long as I felt was needed, I felt to blame for my miscarriage because it all happened through an illness called CMV which caused my waters to break at fifteen weeks.

I wanted to raise awareness of the illness that caused my miscarriage to make people aware of it I wanted to take back the control and to find my inner strength to empower other women to know they are not alone and talking to people about my miscarriage helps others to find the strength to share their story. I shared my miscarriage story on a podcast, and I had messages of gratitude from telling my story which helped me to empower other women to know they aren't alone with a miscarriage. The message I wanted to bring was,

'It's not your fault and there will be a light at the end of the tunnel and your spark will return, it just takes time and to not rush the process. You are strong and you are worthy of having your rainbow baby.' My positive change came from sharing my story.

Since having my miscarriage, I have welcomed my rainbow baby into the world who I am so grateful for. I journaled what I wanted for my future I questioned any of my negative thoughts and rewired them into what I wanted to feel from feeling disempowered to feeling empowered. I found listening to personal development books gave me more self-belief, so I've been able to change the narrative of feeling negative to feeling positive and even though going through a miscarriage was hard I am able to honour my miscarriage and my angel baby lives on within my rainbow baby.

There will always be things that challenge you, but you will find your inner strength and you'll find how you respond to a challenge can help shift your perspective. You will find yourself again by sharing your story you can show people they aren't alone.

I want to empower you to know that you can build your confidence and find your confidence, self-love, and determination. You are worthy and good enough so don't give up until you get what you want to achieve. It's already yours and so what you seek, and desire is always within your reach, you just have to be willing to do the work and take the leap of faith, step out of your comfort zone, and enter the growth zone to watch all the magic unfold to create impact.

ABOUT THE AUTHOR

HANNAH LOUISE BARKER

Hannah is a dedicated mum of four and proud partner of Rob, her journey of self-discovery and empowerment began during the lockdown of 2020. Amidst the challenges of maternity leave and the isolation of the pandemic, she found solace and a renewed sense of purpose through network marketing with The Body Shop at Home. This newfound passion for self-care and skincare

During this transformative period, Hannah also connected deeply with her spiritual side, finding community and support within Facebook groups. Her passion for pole dancing, a beloved activity she has pursued for twelve years, provided her with a physical and emotional outlet, helping her reclaim her spark and energy.

Despite the hardships, including the heartache of three miscarriages, with the most recent one in January 2023, Hannah has faced these challenges with remarkable resilience. Through personal development and a commitment to self-growth, she has transformed negative thought patterns and built a life filled with purpose and positivity. Her journey of overcoming adversity and achieving her goals

She shares her experiences openly, inspiring others to never give up, regardless of setbacks. She is the proud mum of three rainbow babies and believes deeply in the power of crystals, oracle cards, affirmations, and meditation to manifest her desires and goals.

Hannah's mission is to break the cycle of negativity and be the best role model for her children. She demonstrates that anything is possible with resilience, trust, and a positive mindset, encouraging others to pursue their dreams and overcome their own adversities.

You can reach Hannah at:

https://www.facebook.com/share/g/6u2S8Un5eKAULeZ7/?mibextid=K35XfP

BECOMING ME

By Lisa Hardy

At five years old I knew I was here to change the world but growing up in the eighties, my world was one where children should be seen and not heard, and home was no different to that.

We learned very quickly that our thoughts, feelings, and opinions were to be kept to ourselves and speaking up just wasn't an option. It wasn't allowed, and on the rare occasion we tried, we were stopped in our tracks and told it wasn't a good time or they didn't want to hear whinging, as many parents in the eighties did. I became very quickly accustomed to blending into the background and being a 'good girl' and being a twin helped me to hide too.

In school I allowed my sister to take the lead and I happily walked in her shadow. I was a quiet child, rarely raising my hand in class or involving myself in group discussions and even as a teenager I would look in awe at my friends who seemed comfortable with their voices and confident with their words.

As I entered adulthood, the habits formed in childhood became more ingrained. I became a typical people pleaser, always putting other's needs before my own. But being completely honest, I didn't recognise I even had needs. At work I was the go-to person for any task, no matter how inconvenient or challenging. I bent over backwards for clients and colleagues alike, always striving to exceed expectations but despite my hard work and dedication, my efforts were often met with criticism rather than appreciation. Every boss I had seemed to view my keenness and competence as a threat, often accusing me of secretly wanting their job and stepping out of my lane regardless of them happily dumping their additional tasks on me.

The frustration I would feel from being misjudged and mistreated snowballed as I had no way of expressing myself. My throat often felt closed and suffocated, my flimsy attempts to defend myself were dismissed and any objection ignored. If I was ever listened to, my words were twisted, and I was accused of having a chip on my shoulder and a dirty attitude.

The most humiliating instance was when I was handed a disciplinary notice dated the day before I was flying to Spain on my hen do. A disciplinary that was unjustified and had I had the confidence and courage to fight it I would have very easily won. But I didn't, I couldn't, and my boss knew it. The timing was deliberate, a cruel tactic to undermine my happiness which continued until I felt forced to leave two years later.

In another role, I was screamed and spat at whilst being called a f*cking b*tch by a later boss. He asked for my opinion and then refused to let me finish before he was up in my face and you've guessed it, I said nothing, I did nothing... all of which left deep scars, reinforcing my belief that my voice held no value, and my worth was the same.

The need to please unsurprisingly went beyond my professional life. In my personal relationships I found it impossible to say no. I would go to great lengths to avoid disappointing anyone even if it meant sacrificing my own well-being. This immense need to not let people down led to financial instability, getting myself into debt by saying yes to all the things to keep everyone happy.

I became a master of hiding my struggles, I put on a brave face, giving others the best (looking back, potentially fake) version of me whilst inside, everything felt like it was crumbling around me.

The breaking point came when my family and I fell out. I was unable to attend a significant event, no matter which way I tried to make the finances work (including a bank loan) I couldn't, and the backlash was severe. They didn't understand and my apologies, flowers and pleas for empathy and support fell on deaf ears. I understood from their point of view that the timing of my confession could have been earlier but being so unbelievably embarrassed and heartbroken about my situation, I couldn't find the courage. The feeling of isolation and betrayal was overwhelming, it felt like my whole world was collapsing around me and I was powerless to stop it despite my efforts and embarrassing begging for forgiveness.

The fallout with my family marked the beginning of my lowest point ever. The stress and heartache were unbearable, and I found myself being unable to sleep for an entire year. Insomnia took its toll leaving me physically, mentally, and emotionally broken and I became prone to sudden uncontrollable bouts of crying, overwhelmed by the weight of my heartache. Public places, private moments, it didn't matter, the tears came unannounced relentlessly. I felt so invisible, unheard, and completely and utterly alone.

My mental and emotional state deteriorated rapidly. I was consumed by feelings of unworthiness and despair from hurting those that I loved so much. My identity, once being the kind, thoughtful, attentive friend, sister, and daughter now felt further from the truth. I had suddenly lost myself, the person in the mirror felt like a stranger, a mere shadow of who I once was.

During the darkness a small light shone in the form of an Instagram post by Kirsty Gallagher. Her words resonated with me in a way nothing else ever has. She spoke about *Luna living*, a concept that was brand new to me yet felt strangely familiar. Intrigued to know more, I joined her two-hour online yoga and luna musing, something I would never have done before - two hours to myself felt too self-absorbed but I had a deep knowing. I needed this like nothing before and a decision I had no idea would change my life forever.

For the first time in my life, I felt like I'd found home within myself. I finally understood myself and no longer felt different or alone – feelings that had lived daily in my subconscious. The teachings of luna living started to give me a new perspective of life and myself. I began to understand the cycles of the moon and how they influenced my emotions and energy. I soon came to realise that I wasn't weird, I wasn't losing the plot, and this knowledge became empowering, it provided me with a sense of calm, control and understanding of myself that I had never experienced before.

As I delved deeper into the practices of living by the moon, I started to reclaim parts of myself that I had forgotten. I learned to listen to my thoughts and feelings, and I started to understand myself for the first time since I was five. I know this must sound outrageous, but I remember the message as clear as day, "You're here to save the world Lisa" and at that age it didn't feel obscene. Of course, I had no idea how, why, what or when and although throughout the following years the message got lost, subconsciously in my twenties, I began looking for the answer that continued for over twenty years.

Through Kirsty's practices I learned to honour myself and I started to work on my voice both internally and externally. It wasn't a quick or easy process, far from it, it was often dark and terrifying but with each step I felt stronger and a little more put together as I healed. I began to set boundaries, something I'd never dared do before. Saying no not only became an act of self-love, but it also became empowering, it enabled me to stand tall with my head held high, it would fuel my worth and no longer be the source of guilt that would eat me up beyond comprehension.

The changes were not just in me, I started to notice a shift in how others perceived and treated me too. By valuing myself and my needs, I unexpectedly taught others to do the same, I couldn't believe it! I found the courage to speak up, to express my myself slowly and calmly without fear of backlash or punishment. My words once silenced or twisted now flowed with clarity and confidence. Not that it was always easy, old habits naturally die hard but with my new-found life-changing skill of consciousness and the desire to change forever, I found a way. It's now clear to see I lost myself at a very young age. The person I was meant to be was buried under heavy layers of fear, insecurity, and the relentless need to please others. But through the pain, misery and struggles during the hardest time of my life, I found a way back to myself. I discovered a strength and resilience I never knew I had. I learned that my voice does matter and what I have to say holds substance. My needs are valid, and I am worthy of love and respect and those not willing to meet me here, I moved away from. It wasn't easy, some friends I mourned but we had choices and we both made them.

This chapter of my life has been one of transformation and healing. It's been a journey from silence to self-expression, from invisibility to empowerment, I am grateful for that darkest time of my life and every moment of pain because it led me to here. Now I work helping other women do the same and with them I continue to grow, learn, and embrace who that five-year-old girl was here to be.

I am no longer lost, I am found. I am no longer silenced, I am heard.

ABOUT THE AUTHOR

LISA HARDY

Growing up in an era where children were expected to be seen and not heard, Lisa became a natural people pleaser, constantly looking for approval from those around her. In her late teens, this tendency led her into a four-year abusive relationship, but when she finally broke free, Lisa vowed to never settle for less than she deserved.

Determined to uphold her promise, Lisa embarked on a journey of self-discovery. However, her path was soon rife with challenges and over the next two decades, she faced a series of bullying and abusive bosses, each exploiting her kindness and people-pleasing nature. Despite the professional success she achieved, Lisa often found herself undervalued and mistreated in the workplace.

Lisa's experiences highlight the difficulties many women face in breaking free from cycles of abuse, both professionally and personally. Throughout her life, Lisa struggled with her instinct to please others, but her journey is one of growth and self-empowerment and has transformed her passion into a mission working with women to break-free from their own challenges to create healthier, happier futures. Through one-on-one coaching, masterclasses, and group training programmes, she provides the tools and support needed for personal transformation. As a motivational speaker, Lisa shares her journey and insights at numerous events, inspiring others to reclaim their power, self-respect, and the courage it takes to stand up against all forms of abuse. Lisa is passionate about raising much needed funds for domestic abuse charities throughout the UK.

You can reach Lisa at:

www.instagram.com/confidenceandmore

DON'T DREAM IT, BE IT.

By Joanne Lazarus

There was a time, as a family that we decided to pack up and move to Spain to begin a new life, a new adventure. With three children, two teenagers, and a nine-month baby, Ray and I headed off into the Spanish sunset for a new life adventure.

It was an exciting yet nervous time, but in my mind, I had planned how I would spend our school, social and working life. Once we arrived on the sunny Costa Blanca and found a home, being a determined cookie, I took myself off to lessons and threw myself into learning the language as best as I could, so when the children went to school, I could understand what was going on with other parents and the teachers.

I had planned our time in Spain. I had a vision to open my own drama school. The expat community was to hand, and I wanted to give the younger members of the community an outlet where they could enjoy drama in their own language.

I set the wheels in motion and in life before Facebook, it was posters and word of mouth that enabled me to begin my drama school. With feelings of imposter syndrome, I questioned whether I was worthy of opening a drama school. Would I be taken seriously? I had been an actor for thirteen years at that point and wanted to open my own business use the skills that I had acquired as an actor. I opened the doors to the beginnings of what I thought would be a smooth vision of having my own business.

I invited one of the mums, who I had a connection with over the time, to join me as a helper. I noticed her Spanish language skills were excellent and I believed she would be a big help on the admin side. Little did I know at that time, later she would pull the carpet from under me and steal my whole vision and replicate my school whilst dampening my reputation by the form of online bullying to create her own vision of taking over my school.

After various successful projects and shows had been produced, I noticed a change in my friend. Lies were being spread on social media about me. Close members of the expat community found it fit to believe the stories. She had put it out there on Facebook, the new tool, where those who needed to, could use it as an open platform to use bullying tactics. I was soon victim to a group of trolls, spreading the words to dampen my reputation.

I could see groups of people within the area where I lived, making comments about me and my life became intolerable as I found myself the victim of a Facebook bully campaign. How could these stories be believed by some that actually knew me? The straw that broke me, was when she decided to publicly announce that the drama school was closing, and we would be opening another separately. She wrote a letter to hand out to the parents saying that the reason we had decided to part ways, is because I was busy with other projects and had no time to run the drama school any longer. It was an outright lie. This was due to that woman now teaming up with another person who owned a dancing school in the next village. She had support and the two worked together to get me closed. How could she have done this to me? I was heartbroken.

The camaraderie and friendships I had built whilst running the drama school were becoming corrupt. I believed people had to decide which drama school they wanted to attend full stop and the whole thing was beyond my comprehension of anything I had ever experienced in my life.

The amount of controversy and bullying that went on broke me. It broke me more so than anything I had known in the past apart from the time I had lost my father at his young age of forty-nine.

To add to this already awful time, we were going through family financial problems because we had hit the credit crunch of 2008. Life was hard, money was non-existent, and it came to the point we really didn't know if we would lose the house that we'd bought. If was a choice between buying food or paying the electric bill.

The dream life on the Costa Blanca was soon becoming the nightmare of all nightmares not only, was I being emotionally bullied and a victim of ridicule, but we were also nearly having to leave Spain without our home that we had worked hard for.

With great heartache, we took the decision to go back home to Manchester. As Spain was not only breaking us emotionally, but it also was breaking us up as a family. My marriage was failing. Our daughter left to go back to England, and our other daughter moved out of the family home. We had no money, and my drama school business was coming to an end. The people who had bullied me had opened their own drama school, and some of the students went over to them. In the end I gave up the will to care any longer. So, it was great sadness as we left Spain, my inner soul also died within me. I was broken

We rented a small home, as our house was still in Spain, luckily, we managed to rent it out to help pay the mortgage. After everything my entrepreneurial spirit had dwindled, and my inner heart felt like it was in two and my energy had gotten up and gone. It was also a sad time for the family as my husband and myself, after 22 years of marriage, decided to split up.

Back home in Manchester, now living apart, getting my active head back on was hard yet I managed it. A friend, who had a job at the one of the world's biggest football clubs, introduced me to his workplace, where I ended up getting work as a tour guide at Manchester United FC. How did a girl who knew nothing about football get a job as a tour guide there? I felt like an imposter, as I very quickly had to learn about the team. I did enjoy my newly discovered challenge, but was also offered work, as an actor, doing work as a simulated patient for the medical profession so I found myself having to become self-employed due to the acting work. Over the eight years I was at Manchester United FC, I found myself getting busy, as the simulated patient work was getting more frequent, my inner heart was feeling less hurt, and my husband and I had also got back together. Life was beginning to get back to an even keel and life was looking better.

The entrepreneurial spirit began to ooze back into my life. It was making its way back into my heart back into my passion. Even though the drama school bullying was still in my mind, at long last, that spark was returning to me, and I felt ignited, and the spirit of wanting more was back. I was not going to let some jealous business rivals steal my emotions any longer. I was bigger than that. After all, if I can get a job at one of the world's biggest football clubs, without having any football knowledge, the world could open up to overcome my negative emotions. This became the 'new me.' The girl who had her sights on the job she wanted, in a place I never thought I would work. They don't call it the 'Theatre of Dreams' for nothing.

But my dreams didn't stop. They kept on recurring. And as each new idea came to my head, they evolved, so the more empowered me decided I would go into business for myself. Still keeping my days at the stadium, as I loved being there, I used my free time, and the money I was earning from my work, to begin my entrepreneurial stepping stones to my successful life balance. What do I mean by that? I need more than a chapter, but after beginning and failing of new businesses and schemes, (they aren't fails, see? They are stepping stones to success), I have reached my optimum happiness. My work life balance. I am now a celebrant and freelance director of my own work hours and lifestyle. I am a CEO of Joanne Lazarus Celebrant along with advising businesswomen on being their confident upmost self in front of a camera lens.

Do I miss the sunny life in Spain? No, not really, because now we, as a family have grown and can visit there whenever we wish. The two teens have turned into beautiful stunning girls, each with loving partners, and we now have two grandchildren. The nine-month baby boy is now eighteen and has learned to be an independent man who we are so proud of. He was diagnosed with autism, and we as a family, embrace what he brings to us and don't let it get in our way.

Have the attitude to dream big, the attitude to get up when someone kicks you down. Don't listen to the haters, as they do not deserve to live rent free within your emotions. Only you can make you into the person, you want to be.

ABOUT THE AUTHOR

JOANNE LAZARUS

Joanne's story begins with her acting passion began at a very early age. From being the lead in the high school play, to having roles on TV dramas. For thirty years, work life has been acting based with an array of appearing in TV, treading the boards on stage, murder mysteries, teaching drama, being a simulated patient for the medical profession and now passionately, a wedding celebrant. However, a love of drama & teaching is still there.

With a love of travel, especially one for the high seas, many happy years in her twenties were spent sailing the ocean waves working in the tax and duty-free shops on board cruise ships. Joanne felt privileged to have sailed halfway round the world.

Love of travel meant encouraging the family to live in Spain, on the stunning Costa Blanca, where Joanne opened her own drama school. Teaching drama and producing shows for the expat communities. After six years away, Joanne and her family returned to the UK after being caught up in some online bullying and the financial crash of 2008.

Joanne's love for celebrations and her organisational skills during her drama teaching years, brought her to use those skills to open her own wedding event business "JL On the day", and became an on the day wedding coordinator. The pandemic put a stop to large events. Joanne quickly used the time to retrain as a wedding celebrant. Joanne loves being an officiant, helping couples to achieve the wedding ceremony they desire. This is a recent business she has become to love.

Married to Ray a mum of three and loving her new role in life as grandma to two cutie pies. Joanne still loves to travel, is a social butterfly and loves going to the theatre.

You can reach Joanna at:

www.joannelazaruscelebrant.co.uk

FROZEN IN TIME

By Chaz Kafetzis

As the sun dips below the horizon, and I sit gazing through my balcony window I am surrounded by an array of colourful crystal beads, each one sparkling with its own unique energy, and every facet ready to tell its own story. Each bracelet I create is filled with vibrant colours and intricate patterns which are a testament to my creativity and imagination, allowing me the freedom to self-express and use the energies from each crystal bead to channel for my clients.

Personally, creating these bracelets is more than just self-expression as with each crystal bead added, I tap into a deeper part of myself, a part that has been neglected due to the hustle and bustle of adult life. This deeper part shields a younger part of me that had been frozen since that day of trauma. As I add the crystal beads, it is as if each gemstone holds a younger version of myself waiting to be re-discovered, nurtured, loved and unfrozen.

FREEZE

My young soul was stolen that day and remained frozen for so long. I lay there still, gazing through the large window ahead of me with wide innocent eyes. The pane of the glass was the barrier between myself and the world I no longer understood. My mind was clouded, and my thoughts felt like broken shards of glass. I longed to articulate the turmoil within myself, but nothing made sense. I was full of chaos and confusion; too much for a child's body. I lost my voice and all I could see was darkness ahead. My senses were overloaded, I was frightened, lost, alone, and abandoned. Frozen.

Time moved on so quickly, yet I found myself moving in slow motion. The outside world was filled with life, laughter, and chatter. I watched the other children play with muffled sounds; in the background their laughter rang like distant echoes. I was yearning to be normal to join in and play but my body was fighting a demon inside of me, the only way I could silence it was through wiping that memory from my existence. Night-time brought no solace, no respite from what I had encountered. Instead, it only deepened the sense of isolation that threatened to consume me.

From my now adult perspective, I know that a wounded child scarred by trauma carries the weight of their experiences like a burden that is too heavy to carry on their little shoulders. Whether you are bullied into silence, racially attacked, torn apart by the loss or divorce of a parent, or shattered by the echoes of emotional, physical, mental, or sexual abuse your innocence becomes a casualty of the cruel realities of life. This was my reality. Each day a battle was fought in my mind where the wounds of the past bleed into the present, leaving me stranded in pain and uncertainty.

Yet despite the darkness that threatens to come over you, the wounded child will hold onto a glimmer of hope, a flickering flame that refuses to be extinguished, a testament to their resilience to overcome adversity.

LOCKDOWN

Locked down, my world fell silent once more, gripped with fear from an unknown disease ravaging every corner of our earth. Confusion hung heavy in the air as we were barricaded within our homes, cut off from the familiar routines of life. The world looked so different, like an apocalyptic movie where life was so surreal. It didn't feel real. Life came to a standstill. Days stretched into weeks and months. I found myself transported back to a time of innocence, my inner child screaming for answers in a world turned upside down.

Yet, amidst the chaos, my adult self struggled to navigate the storm of emotions raging within me. My relationships with my family were strained under the weight of my silent suffering, my loved ones unable to comprehend my distance, the silence, and the internal war within me. It was my inner child - that vulnerable, frightened younger self, who cried out for understanding and compassion, a pain too familiar happening once again in my adult life.

In the depths of my isolation, I found comfort in unhealthy habits, online shopping to fill that void of being unhappy, drowning my fears and binge eating late-night snacks, staying awake into the early hours as insomnia took over. Deep down, I knew I was only running from the truths I dared not face. Locked in a cycle of avoidance, I had neglected the cracks of my life, until they threatened to crumble beneath me.

At that time, my youngest son's struggles mirrored my own, and became a painful reminder of the ripple effect of my unresolved demons. With newfound clarity and strength, I vowed to confront the shadows lurking in my mind, to reclaim control of my life and guide my son through the storm. I soon realised that it wasn't him that needed guiding, it had been my younger self all along. Locked down, the world may have fallen silent, but within my own soul, a journey of self-discovery and healing was awaiting as I learned to embrace the wounded child within and forge a path towards redemption. A form of hypnosis took place, and I was about to thaw a part of me that became frozen as a child on that day.

MASK OFF

Behind the mask of roles that I was playing - wife, mother, daughter, sister, friend, colleague lurked a wounded child, drowning in a whirlpool of grief and betrayal. I had been in therapy for three years but my progress using conventional therapy seemed to grind to a halt, leaving me stuck in unresolved pain. Whilst hypnosis had unveiled fragments of hidden truths, I was still in search of inner peace, comfort and understanding of myself. My communication was broken as I struggled to piece together my lost childhood.

There was a darkness that overshadowed a small part of my childhood, yet the ripple effect of what had happened played out in years to come. Its effects regurgitated through the years in the form of fear and anxiety, clinging to me like a second skin.

Desperate for solace, I turned to spiritual guidance and holistic treatments. Crystals that were vibrant and radiant filled my space with the light that I needed. They became my companions in the journey towards inner healing by steadying my mind and focusing on the here and now. Their radiant glow illuminated the murky depths of my soul, grounding me in the present moment and forging a path of light in the darkness.

As I became more self-aware, I was in search of answers to make sense of my past – my childhood.

This is when I encountered Judith Hindle, a spiritual medium and mentor, that proved to be the catalyst for my true transformation and acceptance. I was encapsulated by Judith's knowledge, and her spiritual teachings the non-woo way, even more so she understood the depths of my hidden pain. I joined her 'Awakening' programme that took me into the light of spirituality and the true meaning of life. It was here where the mask finally came off.

Under Judith's guidance, I peeled back the layers of my being, confronting each scar and shadow with courage and compassion. Through the modules and workbooks, I learned to unravel the knots of hurt and fear, to accept, release, and forge a path towards healing. With each revelation, I felt the walls around my heart began to crumble, things were starting to make sense, I could now see the bigger picture. My reactive state has now been replaced by unconditional love for myself and the parts of me that have been long neglected and abandoned. Determined to break the cycle of generational trauma, I embraced the journey inwards and the gateway to releasing my frozen inner child began.

NEW BEGINNINGS

Through the lens of my own eyes, I have learned so much about my life. Each day brings new experiences and challenges, and with them, new lessons to unfold. My true connection to the divine, my spiritual awakening, and working with my crystals have all guided me on a profound journey of self-awareness and self-discovery. Every facet of my life, both the good and the bad, has contributed to my growth, shaping me into the person I was then and the person I am now. Through new beginnings came understanding and acceptance, but more so connection to my inner child.

Embracing spirituality has helped me see beyond what is in front of me but revealing the deeper truths within. Crystals with their unique energies and vibrations, have been my companions, illuminating my path and grounding me in the present. Their beauty and power have become my source of strength and clarity, helping me to navigate my complex life. In moments of reflection, I see the tapestry of my life woven with threads of joy and sorrow, triumph, and struggle. These experiences, no matter how painful, have been integral to my growth. They have taught me resilience, compassion, and the importance of self-love.

As I continue to walk this path, I understand that learning is a lifelong journey. Every day is an opportunity to discover something new about myself, to heal another part of my soul, and to embrace the present moment with gratitude. My spiritual learnings and creative practices have become my light through my struggles. Through this journey, I have learned to cherish the child within, to offer her the love and understanding she always deserved. By doing so, I have unlocked a creative part of me that is free and full of joy that had been long suppressed.

Each day, I strive to nurture my inner child, to honour her needs and dreams, and to live a life that is true to myself. In these moments of truth, I may lose connections to my loved ones but create new connections that will elevate me to who I really am. My connections to the divine, the wisdom of my spiritual mentors, and the creative space of using crystals have all played a pivotal role in my transformation of unfreezing that little child within me. They have guided me towards a deeper understanding of who I am and what I am capable of and as I continue to grow, I am committed to embracing every lesson, every challenge, and every moment with an open heart and an open mind.

My story, like each bracelet that I create is intricate and powerful and now with self-compassion and understanding, each gemstone allows me the freedom to self-express so that the energies from each crystal bead can be a channel for my clients and a way to celebrate and share my open heart with theirs.

ABOUT THE AUTHOR

CHAZ KAFETZIS

Chaz is a devoted mother to three beautiful boys. Her struggle with mental health issues intensified during lockdown, as her youngest son struggled to settle into school and her relationships with loved ones came under strain. Therapy revealed unresolved childhood trauma that Chaz had long dissociated from. Finding little solace in conventional therapy, Chaz turned to spiritual and holistic treatments for healing.

In her darkest moments, crystals guided her towards the light. In January 2022, she began studying for an international qualification in Crystal Healing, proudly completing her certification a year later. Throughout her journey, Chaz developed a deep connection to wearing crystal jewellery. The energy from the crystals brought her peace and reminded her of her strength in facing childhood trauma.

In March 2023, Chaz launched a crystal jewellery business, creating handmade custom pieces infused with energy and intentions. Her work has attracted a loyal following on Instagram, including well-known celebrities. Recently, Chaz started a YouTube channel called Creative Gemz, where she teaches her audience to make creative items such as Jewellery, Sun Catchers, and Tree of Life pieces, all infused with healing energies. Chaz's mission is to help people recognise and heal from childhood trauma through creative expression, nurturing their inner child, and embarking on a mindful journey of self-love and healing.

You can reach Chaz at:

https://gemzhealing.com

LIVING THROUGH THE CHANGES IN LIFE

By June Bernard

In the 1980's before we had mobile phones, internet, and social media, I was married to Jock and was a mum bringing up three children Donna, John and Carol doing the best I could. I was very lucky to have a good supportive family to help me but bringing up a family, life can be super busy, leaving your self-care at the bottom of the list. I didn't realise at the time that I suffered with pre-menstrual tension (PMT) which meant in the week leading up to my periods I would get very moody. Nobody told me that this was happening to my body at this time. I didn't have any conversations with my mum about how periods can affect how you feel at that time. I do think It is something that we should as women be talking to each other about.

It wasn't until a work colleague asked me one day if I was getting near the time of the month, I was really shocked that she knew this and asked her how she knew. She then told me that I had PMT, when I heard the words, "You have PMT," this was when I became aware of what I was going through. I had absolutely no control over these emotions and felt really guilty and ashamed of my actions. I didn't realise before just how bad I was, it would only take for someone to say something that would trigger an anger and I would start shouting at them. Afterwards I would feel so annoyed and embarrassed at myself. It must have been very hard for my family living with me during those weeks.

I can now look back at my life and see how I reacted to simple things that people would say to me. It wasn't a nice feeling having no control over my emotions especially when it was also affecting other people. I didn't know anyone else that was suffering with PMT, so I felt that I was the only person to have this. I am not a person that likes to go to the doctors unless I am really unwell, I now wish I had gone and got some help with this hormone imbalance that was going on in my body. I don't want my grown-up daughters feeling this way, so we do talk about it together.

Going into perimenopause was a lot easier for me, with the previous symptoms as my periods started to miss a good few months until I finally stopped getting them and the premenstrual tension storms were finally gone.

When I went into menopause my weight increased to the heaviest, I had ever been in my life. I had been a yo-yo dieter for most of my life after having my children. I tried most of the diet fads that were on the go at the time. I remember doing a three-day juicing diet, where you put fruit and vegetables into the juicer and just drank these throughout the day. On the morning of day two I had the worst headache with the detox, you were only meant to drink water, but that morning I had a cup of tea. I now feel angry and disappointed that I let my body image have such control of my emotions with food.

I joined a weight loss class, and I would get to my target weight, it did feel good to get that bell to ring and everyone in the room would clap for you. The support was great the night of your weigh in, but then it was up to you to stick to the eating habits they were teaching you the rest of the time. The only down fall with the location of the club was that it was across the road from the chippy, what do you think happened? Yes, you guessed right if I had a good weight loss, I would reward myself with something to eat that night on the way home. I think the worst times for me was when I was in the house on my own or at night when my children had gone to bed. I would just eat whatever snacks that were in the cupboards out of boredom.

When I was overweight, I would do my best to try and avoid getting my picture taken, I do regret this now as I like to look back at my memories. It was at the point when I started to get problems with acid reflux, and I could feel my breathing was starting to get affected that I knew I had to do something to keep my weight under control. By this time, I had become a granny and wanted to be able to run around and play games with my grandchildren.

I know now that these were all part of lessons of life, that were needed to help me move forward making me resilient, grateful, inspired, and proud of what I have achieved so far on my journey of self-love.

I was introduced to personal development in my fifties by two lovely ladies who were running a weight loss programme. I joined my first network marketing company with them. I was encouraged to read books and start working on myself. This is when I started to make myself a priority and took time for some self-care. I began to exercise and started to do a couch to 5k as I had signed up to do a 5k run with some family members for charity. It was good to encourage, support each other and to celebrate achieving our first run together. I built up on my running by going out two to three times a week and signed up with a friend to do my first half marathon at Edinburgh.

I had to go out running more and had to start a plan to build up the km so that I would be able to run this half marathon. Some days I would do shorter runs and one day a week I would do a long run which I would increase each week. The training was quite tough, and I had to keep a strong mind to keep going, but I also didn't want to let my friend down. If it is easier going out with Lynne and Lesley who I first met at a fit camp, we all attended together and with my daughter Donna.

On the day of the half marathon, it was so exciting to get there and there was a fantastic atmosphere. During the run everybody was so supportive and there were lots of people standing in the streets cheering us on and some were handing out Jelly babies to help give us a little sugar boost. I was so happy to reach the finish line and receive my medal. It felt amazing to achieve this. In that moment I felt so empowered and proud of myself.

I now like to continue with my personal development and work on myself every day. I have found that joining communities of positive women all working towards our goals is very inspiring and supportive. Earlier this year I signed up to do a journaling mission run by Lisa Williams - The Vision Board Queen. I was encouraged to start by linking my journal into a habit that I already done, I decided first thing in the morning would be the best time while I was enjoying my first cup of tea of the day. I got myself some cards which give me prompts which I needed to get me started. I have a focus deck five minutes in the morning and a set of oracle cards, moon magic book and card deck. With the cards I shuffle them and look at the card on top that is what I will journal on that morning, the moon cards I use to check I am on the right path towards my goals. Journaling each morning is really helping me get to know myself better and I can work through any problems that arise during the day.

Working through getting to know myself better I have stopped dieting and replaced it with making better choices, as I realised that being healthy and keeping up my fitness is more important to me, and I have learned to be happy in my body. I have become more confident with my journaling and before I would never have considered to be writing a chapter in a book collaboration with twenty-seven other inspiring women. I hope by writing this chapter that it helps you in your life moving forward and to know that you can change your life.

I am now very grateful that I was encouraged to read books to help me with my personal development the first books I read were, The Secret by Rhonda Byrne and Think and Grow Rich by Napoleon Hill, these books taught me how to start thinking in a more positive way. If you are just starting to work on your personal development journey, I would recommend starting with these two books. Being part of a community of like-minded people will give you connections with others who will help and support you on your journey.

I would love to know how you get on using any of the tools that I have mentioned in this chapter to help you on your journey of self-love. You can find me on Facebook in my group, 'Shimmer and Shine with June, self-care, and well-being.' Start to work on yourself and you will see the changes it will bring you. Looking back on my earlier years I did not have a lot of confidence in myself, and I would stop myself from believing I could achieve things in life. I am grateful that I worked on myself to grow through personal development, using the tools I recommended in this chapter.

ABOUT THE AUTHOR

JUNE BERNARD

June is married, has three grown up children and is a Gran. She worked as a nursing assistant for twenty-four years. She now spends more time with her family. June lived with PMT symptoms most of her life. She feels this is something that should be talked about to help women know they are not struggling with this alone.

In 2014 June was introduced to network marketing and started on her personal development journey. She started to work on her mindset, learning to lead a more positive life. She was encouraged to read books to help her grow as a person.

June now likes to run and has achieved two half marathons which she raised money for two charities, cancer research and SAMH. June also likes to go out walking, reading, knitting, crochet and making cards.

In February 2024 June started to journal every morning to work on her journey of self-love. Through journaling she is getting to know herself better and what her true values are. June uses journaling in her daily life to work through any problems that arise throughout her day.

June is passionate to encourage women to take time for themselves and to relax and to get creative making cards. June runs two Facebook groups, 'Shimmer and Shine with June- self-care and wellbeing.' and 'Crafty June Bernard.'

You can reach June at:

www.facebook.com/groups/1999641263505239

THE STRENGTH IN THE STRUGGLE

By Joanne Gibson

In my early years, finding inspiration and motivation was difficult. My childhood was filled with constant turmoil, and my home, which should have been a place of comfort, felt more like a challenging environment. I often felt unworthy and unloved, compounded by the lack of support from those around me.

Fear and anxiety were my constant companions. Each day was unpredictable, and I never knew what might happen next. This left me feeling deeply insecure. I longed for a sense of routine, a place to feel safe and valued. These experiences profoundly impacted my self-esteem and how I viewed the world.

My school wasn't any better. Being labelled as the 'poor girl,' I was an easy target for bullies. Their taunts and cruelty only reinforced my belief that I was different and undeserving of kindness. I still remember the sting of their words and the loneliness I felt as I navigated the schoolyard alone. I often wondered why I couldn't fit in or be accepted for who I was.

STRUGGLES WITH IDENTITY: AUTISM AND ADHD

As I grew older, I faced new challenges that eventually led me to find my inspiration. It wasn't until I was an adult that I finally acknowledged that I was neurodiverse; I finally understood how aspects of my behaviour were due to autism spectrum disorder (ASD) and attention deficit hyperactivity disorder (ADHD). This revelation was both a relief and a challenge! On one hand, it explained the struggles and feelings of inadequacy that had followed me since childhood. On the other hand, it highlighted the difficulties of living in a world not designed for neurodiverse individuals.

To cope, I learned to wear a mask, hiding my true self to meet the expectations of society. This constant effort to fit in was exhausting and took a significant toll on my mental health. The bullying I endured in school left deep scars, making self-acceptance even harder. I was always pretending to be someone I was not, just to survive in a world that seemed determined to reject me.

Discovering my neurodiversity was a revelation. It helped me understand many aspects of my personality and behaviours that had previously been sources of shame or confusion. More importantly, it connected me with a broader community of individuals who shared similar experiences. This sense of belonging was a lifeline, a beacon of hope in a world that often felt isolating. It showed me that I wasn't alone in my struggles and that a supportive network of people understood and accepted me for who I was.

TURNING POINT: SUPPORT FROM NAN

Amidst all this, my nan (known as Edna) was my beacon of hope. She saw my potential and encouraged me to believe in myself. Her unwavering support gave me the courage to pursue higher education, something I had never thought possible given my background and the self-doubt that had been instilled in me from a young age.

With her encouragement, I enrolled in university and eventually became a teacher. This was a monumental achievement for me, not just academically but personally. It was a step towards reclaiming my life and building a future I could be proud of. My nan's belief in me was the spark that set me on a path of self-improvement and empowerment.

Edna's lessons were not just about academics. She taught me the importance of self-respect and perseverance. Her wisdom and kindness were like a soothing balm to my wounded soul, giving me the strength to push forward even when things seemed impossible. Her influence on my life was immense; she was my anchor and the light that guided me through my darkest times.

Edna's home was a sanctuary for me. I fondly remember sitting with her, drinking 'proper' coffee, and listening to her life stories. Her presence was a constant source of comfort and stability. She had a way of making me feel valued and important, something I rarely felt elsewhere.

Her belief in me helped me develop a sense of self-worth that I had never experienced before, empowering me to embrace my true self and not just survive but thrive in a world that had once seemed determined to reject me.

BEING AN AUTISTIC MUM

Raising five children as an autistic mother had its unique challenges and rewards. My need for routine and structure heavily influenced my parenting style. My children always had a shower before bed, meals were meticulously planned, and we often ate the same foods for months at a time. This predictability provided a sense of stability and security for my children.

However, there were times when I experienced ADHD/autism burnout. During these periods, maintaining our usual routines became impossible. Dinners would consist of cereal or takeout, and I felt dysregulated and stressed, mistaking these feelings as depression. It was a delicate balance, but my dedication to providing a stable environment for my children never wavered. I found ways to manage these periods by seeking support from loved ones and allowing myself the grace to step back and recharge.

Being an autistic mum meant finding creative solutions to everyday challenges. I developed systems and routines that worked for our family, ensuring that my children felt secure and supported. Despite the occasional setbacks, my love for my children and commitment to their well-being was unwavering. I learned to embrace my unique strengths and use them to create a nurturing and loving home.

RAISING NEURODIVERSE CHILDREN

My children are all neurodiverse, each with their unique strengths and challenges. My oldest is a gifted child with ADHD; two are on the autism spectrum, another only has ADHD, and my youngest has sensory and auditory processing disorders. Navigating their needs requires patience, understanding, and a lot of advocacy.

My training, qualifications, and experiences have equipped me to support them effectively. I've adapted my approach to meet each child's needs, ensuring they receive the care and support necessary to thrive. This journey has been challenging and rewarding, providing me with profound insights into how neurodiversity can manifest. I've learned to celebrate their differences and help them harness their unique abilities.

Raising five very different neurodiverse children has been an eye-opening experience. It has taught me the importance of flexibility, empathy, and perseverance. Each of my children has their own unique way of seeing the world, and they have enriched my life in countless ways. The challenges we've faced together have strengthened our bond and deepened my understanding of neurodiversity.

We've had our share of struggles, but we've also experienced many joys. Watching my children grow and thrive has been one of the most significant rewards of my life. They've taught me to see the world through different lenses and appreciate diversity's beauty. Their resilience and creativity inspire me every day.

WHEN LIFE MAKES YOU STOP, PAUSE AND REASSESS

Despite my many successes, I eventually found myself struggling again.

In 2014, I went through early menopause, which no one picked up on; it brought a range of complex physical and emotional symptoms that I had to navigate. On top of that, I also developed a rare autoimmune disease, myasthenia gravis, that went undiagnosed for a long time. I had MRIs and many, many hospital appointments to see why I had constant double vision, loss of voice, limited breathing, choking and chronic fatigue. My life hit rock bottom; the combination of these health issues and my neurodiversity made daily life a constant struggle, testing my resilience and determination.

The journey to diagnosis was filled with frustration and uncertainty. The lack of understanding and recognition of my symptoms by medical professionals only added to my struggles. However, once I did my own research and proved that I had myasthenia gravis, even though I didn't present as a typical patient, I was finally diagnosed; I could seek the proper treatment and support, which significantly improved my quality of life. Finding the right healthcare professionals who understood my condition was a turning point. They provided me with the tools and strategies to manage my symptoms and improve my overall well-being.

Managing health issues added another layer of complexity to my life. Dealing with the symptoms and advocating for my health needs required a deep well of strength and resilience. This experience taught me the importance of self-care and prioritising my well-being, lessons that have been invaluable in my journey. I learned to listen to my body and make choices that supported my health, even if it meant making difficult decisions.

In 2019, I returned to the UK due to my autoimmune disease and the frustration of working long hours in a department that wasn't neurodiverse-friendly. The demands of the job, coupled with the lack of understanding and accommodation for my neurodiverse needs, took a toll on my health and well-being. I realised that I needed to prioritise my health and find a work environment that was supportive and inclusive.

Back in the UK, I had the chance to rebuild my life and start a new chapter. The move was both challenging and liberating. I had to adapt to the changes and uncertainties, but I also saw it as an opportunity to create a life aligned with my values and aspirations. The support of friends and family in the UK played a crucial role in my transition. They helped me to navigate the complexities of my health condition and encouraged me to pursue my dreams.

I started my own small business, focusing on helping other small business owners, parents of neurodiverse children, and individuals who need understanding and strategies to move forward. This new venture has allowed me to use both my qualifications and my lived experiences to help others, providing them with the support and knowledge I once longed for.

Building my business has been incredibly fulfilling. It has given me the opportunity to connect with others who share similar challenges and to make a positive impact in their lives. I offer practical advice, emotional support, and personalised strategies to help them navigate their unique situations.

I've learned that life is a journey filled with ups and downs, but how we navigate these challenges defines us. My experiences have shaped me into who I am today, and I am grateful for the lessons they have taught me. I am passionate about using my story to inspire and support others, helping them find their own paths to success and happiness.

Reflecting on my journey, I see a tapestry woven with threads of hardship, resilience, and triumph. From a childhood marked by turmoil to an adulthood defined by self-discovery and advocacy, my life is a testament to the power of perseverance. Today, I am positive, inspired, and motivated. My story is one of transformation, showing that no matter the obstacles, it is possible to overcome and thrive. I have definitely demonstrated my strength in my struggle.

ABOUT THE AUTHOR

JOANNE GIBSON

Despite enduring significant adversity, Joanne's story is a testament to the power of resilience. Growing up in a tumultuous environment, where home was more of a battlefield than a sanctuary, Joanne was surrounded by feelings of unworthiness and neglect. Fear and anxiety were her constant companions, shaping an unpredictable world that chipped away at her self-esteem. At school, she was often labelled as the 'poor girl', a target for bullies, which left her feeling isolated and struggling with her identity. Yet, through it all, Joanne's resilience remained unwavering.

Embracing her neurodiversity connected her with a community that celebrated individuality and diversity. This sense of belonging and acceptance provided hope and a new perspective, highlighting the power of unity in overcoming challenges.

Throughout her journey, Joanne found unwavering support in her nan, Edna, whose belief in her inspired her to pursue higher education. Joanne's dedication and hard work paid off, as she not only excelled but also earned a master's degree in Learning and Behaviour, a testament to her academic prowess and determination. Today, Joanne runs a successful Neuroinclusive consultant and specialist business that empowers small business owners. Her business offers a range of services, from neurodiversity training for staff to creating inclusive work environments. She also works with parents of neurodiverse children, offering guidance, advice, and evidence-based strategies to help them thrive.

You can reach Joanne at:

www.neuroinclusiveconsultant.co.uk

THE FREEDOM OF CHOICE

By Joanne Cook

At the age of thirteen I was asked by a male relative, "Do you want to be an accountant or a mum?" Why was I being defined already at thirteen? I still feel anger from this outdated question. Society often seeks to define us before we've had a chance to define ourselves. If only I could reach out to my thirteen-year-old self and call out this utter nonsense and remind her that she is not confined to the narrow choices imposed upon her.

As I turned twenty-one, a male CEO at an interview asked me, "Will you be having children?" Surely this had no relevance to the job. I was being defined as a woman again, a question that I was confident men were not being asked. I justified why I wanted to focus on a career and had not thought about having children. I wanted to be successful in my career, live the city life and have everything that I had dreamed of, I wanted to achieve so much more. I questioned if this was truly possible as it seemed I would need to decide at some point whether I wanted to exchange all of this to become a mum.

I began to doubt my choices because that CEO made me feel limited in my choices. Imagine the countless women who, like me, have sat across from potential employers, only to be questioned about their plans for motherhood instead of their skills and qualifications. How many amazing, capable women have been made to feel that their career ambitions are somehow secondary, that they must justify their professional goals?

At twenty-two I gave birth to my first son. Two lines on a pregnancy test that I had not planned to see at that point. I stayed in a job that I didn't enjoy receiving maternity pay. As I entered motherhood, questions began to turn into assumptions. It was clear that others had expected me to naturally give up my career to become a full-time mum, something that I had never planned to do. I continued to justify to people, even before they had asked a question. I felt like I had failed and was proving society right that it was impossible to have a career as a mum. I felt pressured to be more ambitious to prove that I could have both, at times, I would tell people what they wanted to hear but deep down my son really was my priority.

Having an ambitious career was a choice. I got to choose which choices I made, yet I always ended up feeling guilty whatever I chose. The struggle and the juggle are real, not just externally, but emotionally too. I was part of society's beliefs that women stayed at home to raise the children. Something which for generations became the norm. I realised how true this was as I returned to work. Although women are encouraged to move up the corporate ladder, only childless women were achieving this. Motherhood had limited this progression. The pressure of balancing a job and a child was near impossible - something always had to be sacrificed which made me feel more guilty than ever. Women who climbed the career ladder had acquired a sense of masculine ambition and drive, working long hours, proving their dedication. I couldn't compete with this as a mum. Balance did not exist, only increasing amounts of guilt. Whilst at work, I felt guilty for not being at home, and at home, I felt guilty for not working late.

At twenty-two, I realised women are defined by society. It was near impossible to find a way to make it work. I was judged, made to feel selfish and wrong for having a child at twenty-two (all by people who really didn't know me). Surely at twenty-two even though I was a mum, I still had a choice. I could still dream big and get to choose what I wanted? Why had I spent months with a career officer at school asking me what I wanted to be, if being a mum was going to limit my choices?

I realised that the corporate world was not for me as a career mum, I no longer wanted to constantly feel pressured. After having my second son, I pivoted careers, which helped.

As I entered my thirties, balancing motherhood within a leadership role began to have familiar challenges. I had to work even harder to have it all. I'd learned to autopilot life; some would call me super mum for attempting to balance mum life. I was tired and emotionally exhausted. The older the boys became, the more guilt I felt. I would compensate for long working hours with holidays and gifts to justify to myself that I could balance it all. I was trying to be perfect and in control which caused me to burn out twice.

It was in my thirties that I noticed how connected I started to feel with my intuition, and I became determined to break through these barriers. I began to listen to my intuition, stop worrying what others had to say and connect with myself again. I made choices that were right for me. I felt *free* to be the mum I wanted to be and moved on to start my own business, 'Connect with Jo' at the age of forty-one.

At forty-one, married with two sons and two successful careers behind me, I realised more than ever that I did have choices. I did not let the expectations within society continue to define me. I released the expectations of others and the feeling of guilt; I began to feel *empowered*. I no longer needed to be in control, I had choices each day. I began to work on myself and give myself the time I desired. I became more present in the moment each day. I wanted to help other women lead life on their terms and overcome society's barriers. I wanted other women to feel confident that they have choices.

I realised that these societal expectations were there to help you stay safe, play small. Expectations were born from fear of the unknown and generations of following the same patterns as other women. How dare the same societal expectations of our ancestors continue to limit women in today's society where women are rising and no longer wishing to play small. It infuriates me that I spent years worrying what others had thought of me, justifying my decisions, and questioning myself. Why are women of today still having to prove having children does not define their career path and still feeling guilty in having both?

We see changes in society with each year that passes by changes to legislation, equal pay and new opportunities being created. However, the expectations of women having to juggle careers and motherhood are still there. They make sacrifices. They become people pleasers by nature and emotionally drained, losing who they truly are each day. This must stop. Women deserve to rise to their potential, and not have to lose their identity because they chose to have children. It frustrates me that societal expectations are influencing women's choices, causing them to lose their identity after having children. It becomes a fight to succeed. All of which I had felt and have seen may others feel too.

There are women out there who are choosing not to have children and focus on their career, who are experiencing judgement from others and having to work that little harder to prove that they get to choose. Women's age is defined by fertility numbers, adding pressure as women reach milestones. Women are being defined by time when they do and when they don't make choices.

Something must change. This pressure of expectations that is imposed on women of all ages, is stopping women from reaching their potential. Stopping them from living fulfilled lives of freedom. I blame the patriarchy and generations of oppression for women having to question their choices and follow what others deem as right. Ask yourself, is there truly a right or wrong way to live life?

In founding 'Connect with Jo' I knew it would be more than a business. I wanted to create change. I had read that a study had found that women only reach 46% of their potential. This is heartbreaking. Imagine telling your child that they could be less than half of what they wanted to become. *This is so disempowering.* Something must change and it's time that every woman takes back their power and believes more in themselves. Workplaces need more support for working mums to help them not feel guilty in balancing motherhood. Women need to lean into their intuition to make choices that are right for them. Collectively as women we need to free ourselves of anything holding us back.

There will always be expectations and other people's perspectives, but, when you decide to make unapologetic choices for you, your life becomes more fulfilling. So, whether you are thirteen, twenty-two or forty, remember that you always have choices and you get to choose.

Take a moment to ask yourself, ‘what do you want?’ write it down, say it out loud. Now, ask yourself ‘what do you REALLY want?’. Notice how you free yourself from your own limitations in a few minutes.

What action can you take today, next week and next month to start creating the change you want to see? Everything starts with a simple step. The moment you decide to change your perspective, follow your heart, and give yourself permission to have the life you desire.

When it comes to creating your life path, everything is determined by a choice you make and the action that you take. Every choice has a consequence and if you make the choice that is right for you there will never really be a wrong choice. Let’s face it, seeing those two lines at twenty-one were not down to anything other than a choice I had previously made.

Life is not about settling for anything less than what you desire, it is about making choices and acting every day to create a life that lights you up and one that offers you fulfilment.

Be the child within you that dares to dream and the adult who makes it happen.

So go and be that girl who puts buttercups under her chin and smiles at the glow. Who looks up to the blue clear sky with limitless in her eyes and whose heart is full of possibilities that she can and will become anything she truly desires ... because that girl is looking right back at you every time you look into the mirror. She is waiting for you to give yourself full permission to live life on your terms.

ABOUT THE AUTHOR

JOANNE COOK

Joanne Cook is the founder of Connect with Jo. A fully accredited Intuitive Leadership & Legacy Mentor; Joanne combines business strategy with intuitive guidance to help empower women to amplify their impact and create a living legacy.

In July 2002, Joanne gave birth to her first son at the age of twenty-two. Always driven by success and ambition, Joanne began to realise the challenges women faced in today's society balancing a career whilst raising a family. Married to her childhood sweetheart of twenty-seven years, and now a mum of two growing up sons, Joanne understands the unique challenges women face in balancing personal and professional aspirations.

Joanne has navigated her way from the corporate world and pivoted her career into the education sector. In 2018, Joanne saw the beginnings of her third burnout, something that had become the result of living life and running a business on autopilot. Her intuition guided her to follow her spiritual path and purpose, where she made the decision to leave the business that she had successfully grown and later the financial security of full-time employment, turning her focus onto growing her own business, 'Connect with Jo.'

Joanne is passionate about helping women to create more freedom in their lives and their business, enabling them to achieve their dreams with confidence and authenticity. Joanne believes that every woman has the power to shape her own destiny and live a life of purpose and fulfilment.

Connect with Jo helps women through 1:1 and group life and business mentoring sessions, and her free community.

You can reach Joanne at:

www.connectwithjo.com

DELICATE

LEANNE BOWER

As a child, I almost imagined that being married meant being with someone for life. I thought that you made promises that you'd stay together, working as a team and being happy. When I met my now ex-husband, those promises were made before we went down the aisle and said them in front of our family and friends in 2003. We had three beautiful children together and there were times when I genuinely thought we had it all.

During the last few years of my marriage, I'd cry in the bath and wonder whether I'd ever actually be happy again and in 2018, my almost fifteen-year marriage ended. I went through a difficult divorce and the man that I'd refused to see when I was married could be denied no more. The realisation that I'd been in an abusive marriage was something that took me a while to accept. I'd made excuses until there were no more to make and I couldn't ignore what the professionals were telling me any longer. The children and I settled into our own way of doing things and for five years, our home was happy, and we could laugh at the simplest things.

After the divorce and during the healing process, it occurred to me that what had seemed like the most awful thing that could happen was one of the best. I'd thought when we first separated that I was experiencing the worst pain imaginable; however, the worst was yet to come.

There was a period of healing, of finding my worth and of learning to love myself unconditionally. I grieved, I forgave, I started living again and I planned my future. The happiness and peace I felt after my divorce was at times euphoric and other than a couple of areas of my life that I was still working on, I loved my life. This was a feeling that I hadn't thought was possible.

After I'd healed from my divorce, I felt that I'd been given a new purpose. Healing had been an ordeal and I'd had to figure it all out by myself. In doing so, I'd discovered that I could help others. I realised that I could be the guide that I'd needed during that time. I wanted to help other women who had stayed in relationships because they'd had no self-worth or who felt stuck and couldn't move forward. That's when *The Divorce Butterfly* was born.

One February evening in 2023, I missed a call and almost five years after my marriage ended my whole world turned upside down, back to front and inside out. My son wasn't coming home. I never expected it, though perhaps I should have done looking back now but hearing that one of my children wasn't coming home from their dad's was a shock. The reasons that followed were even more surprising. I felt my stomach drop. I felt my heart in my mouth. I tried to process what I was being told.

My eldest son had previously had a difficult relationship with his dad, but he never chose not to go and see his dad. I thought that my son's relationship with both of us was important to him and I respected that wholeheartedly, but it became clear that he no longer wanted anything to do with me. After ending the call and speaking to my parents, I messaged my son and told him that I respected his wishes. Unfortunately, the reasons that I had been given for him leaving meant that my son had told lies about me and my relationship with him and I was sickened that he felt that he needed to do this to achieve the outcome that he wanted. I knew straight away that I'd lost him. That he wouldn't be coming to see me every other weekend as he had his dad when he lived with me. He didn't respond to messages nor answer my call. I gave him space, but I was worried that in doing so, I was giving him space to only think of the negatives that had been created of me and he'd forget who I really was.

The impact of him leaving was far greater than me losing my son. His younger brother took it hard and thought that people left because of him. Then, as he's an intelligent boy, he started to put things together and didn't like the conclusions that he was coming to. It impacted on my daughter and my wider family too. Then came the realisation that my youngest son and I were going to have to move home and that my financial situation had changed drastically. Within the space of six weeks, we'd moved house to live with my partner and either sold, given way, or thrown away the whole life that I'd worked so hard to build for my children and I.

I felt robbed.

Robbed of the excitement I should have been able to feel when I was making such a big step in my relationship by moving in with my partner. How could I be excited when the event that had led up to it was losing my son?

Robbed of what I called the *in between.* These were the years that I'd planned for the children and I, in between us leaving the family home when the divorce was finalised and the time when I would eventually live with my partner.

Robbed of the time that I'd lost with my son. Since becoming a mother, my life had happily revolved around my children and now I was missing out on milestones and moments that I could never get back. It felt like he had died. He was there one minute and then gone the next. At the time of writing, he still is and any hope that I had that that might change is slowly disappearing. I have had to accept that if someone chooses to live their life without you in it, there's not a lot you can do. You must cherish the memories and find a new way to be happy, even though there's a part of you missing. The door is always ajar, but you don't have it wide open because it's like opening the doors in the summer, hoping for the sun to come out, but instead it's freezing, blowing a gale, and hammering down. Hope can be the most glorious feeling in the world, yet it can also bring the most crushing pain.

With the door ajar, I've used the tools that I used to get through my marriage breakdown to help me to get through this. One thing I knew was that I would get through it and there's a light at the end of the tunnel. I didn't lose my sense of self throughout this ordeal and that was my strength. I knew my worth, that I'd done everything I could as a mother, and that I deserved to be happy. I knew that my other children deserved a happy mum, and I also knew that, should the day ever come that my caring, loving, funny boy should ever decide that he wanted his mum to be in his life again, he deserved the best version of me too.

Unfortunately, because I needed the space to heal after my son left, *The Divorce Butterfly* had to be put on hold but then I came back stronger. *The Divorce Butterfly* became a part of a much bigger vision to empower women and children to have the confidence to create their future. *Empowered Futures Ltd* was born incorporating divorce coaching, creating a safe space for mums to support one another as parents and as women, tutoring services for children and eventually helping me to realise my big dream of setting up a social enterprise to support children and tweens whose parents are no longer together.

I've created a membership for mums to help them deal with the overwhelm of running a home, being the default parent and perhaps working outside of the home. I want other women to recognise that learning to look after themselves and loving themselves means that they will have more confidence in how they are as a mum. Removing that constant negative mindset of not being good enough is empowering and you have more fun in the process.

I've created and run several different courses that show women how they have the strength to move forward after heartbreak and give them the tools for whatever stage they are at. These include handling difficult co-parenting situations based on both my first-hand experience and the knowledge I've gained from working with others.

Here are some tips to help you through what feel like your darkest times:

Journal Use this to brain dump before going to bed. It helps to remove things that don't need to be there and give your subconscious space to work on the important things whilst you sleep.

Gratitude Start your day by writing down or saying at least three things you have in your life to be grateful for. This helps to keep your energy higher. We all have things to be grateful for but it's easy for us to forget when we feel low.

Self-Love Work on self-love every day. You have to love yourself at least as much as you want other people to love you and you need to recognise your worth. Once you do these things, your outlook will change, and you'll start to make steps to take control of the things that you can control.

Remember there is always light at the end of the tunnel. You are far stronger than you give yourself credit for.

Now I am looking to a new version of my future and the dream to set up the social enterprise has been with me for a while, long before my son went to live with his dad. I wanted to do this because my children needed support and there just isn't enough of it available. My son was put on a waiting list for counselling in 2019 and in 2024, it has still not been offered. Now I'm even more convinced that this is necessary. It's inspired me and made me further determined to set this up for young people. Creating this space for young people will help to break the cycle of adults being in abusive relationships due to issues born from their own parents' relationships.

Out of the worst event that has happened in my life, I've become a stronger person. I've developed my business so that I can use my experience and expertise to help more people. I'm getting the necessary skills to be able to set up a dream. I choose to focus on these things alongside enjoying time with my nearest and dearest. Should my son decide that he wants his mum in his life again, he'll be met with someone who in his absence, inspired herself to do more and work on herself to become the best version of herself.

ABOUT THE AUTHOR

LEANNE BOWER

Leanne, mum of three and step mum of two, first started her business journey in 2020 during the first COVID 19 lockdown. As a primary teacher, she had previously tutored children to give them confidence and recognise their own abilities and skills.

After her difficult marriage coming to an end, Leanne has spent time working on healing herself and examining why she had made some of the choices that she had in her marriage. Once she recognised the strength within herself and with a firm belief that everything happens for a reason, she decided that she would support other women who were dealing with heartbreak so that they could take control of their futures.

Her life changed drastically once again when her eldest son suddenly left the family home to live with his dad and decided he no longer wanted a relationship with her- an event that was to test all the skills she'd used in her previous healing journey. For a brief period, she found herself questioning her role as a mum and quickly turned things around to once again use this devastating event to create something positive.

She created Empowered Futures Ltd in 2023, encompassing her skills as a teacher, divorce coach and a mum to empower women and children to take control of their futures.

You can reach Leanne at:

www.empoweredfuturesltd.com

I'M STILL STANDING

By Amy Ireland

I am so grateful for where I am today. Despite the trials and tribulations of life like a tree I will always find a way to persevere, regrow and re-generate and that is what I have done all my life. I stand here in 2024 as a successful businesswoman, and mother to four beautiful children. I have a home that has been refurbished because I have found that a fresh environment promotes a healthier headspace. I've also found my significant other. I have a partner who compliments my life and fits in beautifully with my children. This has been a long-standing dream and I have finally met that person who supports me emotionally and physically. I knew I would meet someone one day I wasn't expecting to find someone in February 2024, but life always changes no matter how much you plan. I've realised that love consists of all the small things that show how someone truly cares, and I'm incredibly happy that my life is where it is now. This wasn't always the case, so I'd like to share an insight into my journey from the events that affected me and made me who I am today.

When I was fifteen my life took a turbulent turn when my parents divorced. My mum and brother moved in with my gran, my sister moved in with her boyfriend's parents and I stayed living with my dad and our dog Dana. I struggled with the divorce and mentally, I wasn't in a good place. I began hanging out with the wrong crowd and indulged in drinking. One fateful night in 1990 I attended a party that significantly changed my outlook on life. Alone and in the middle of nowhere, I had a bad encounter that resulted in rape followed by a miscarriage eight weeks later. As a child, I was emotionally torn apart, with little support to process those events and as a result dark thoughts consumed me, and I attempted to take my own life. Thankfully, I received medical assistance just in time and was sectioned in a mental health facility for three months. During that time, I battled with depression and anxiety and struggled to cope with the trauma of what had occurred and understanding why.

Within four years I started to heal and trust again, and I met with a guy who was my age who made me fall for him in a big way by love bombing me daily. I was young, only eighteen at the time, and completely head over heels. Within a month of us being together I fell unexpectedly pregnant which was a huge shock as I was on the pill. Things then became intense, and we moved in together and he became very different and verbally hostile and then violent. I was trapped with this narcissist who made me feel like it was all my fault by saying I made him do it with my behaviour. Due to his manipulation, I felt trapped, lonely, scared, and confused. How could someone who I thought loved me make me feel so worthless and insignificant with his actions?

As a result of his physical aggression, I suffered Meniere's disease, an inner ear imbalance which was bought on by the trauma he put me through and has left me 95% deaf in my left ear. There is no cure and I now accept this as part of my life experience and journey. During this time, we also had another child who I had to fill the void of non-love received from my partner and tried to save the relationship as I couldn't see it for what it really was. Twenty-six years later I don't regret having him for a second and he is one of my four greatest achievements in life.

I eventually summoned the courage to break free but in retaliation he tried to take my children from me, and as the court date approached, I contemplated suicide again. Luckily my cousin saved me from jumping off a sea wall. My husband didn't show up at court, and the judge decided that it would not be in the children's best interest to be near their father due to his actions toward me and for the safeguarding of the children and myself an injunction was served. I was living alone with my children in Burnham and started to rebuild my life and started to believe in myself again.

In 2004 I was finally divorced I was free again, living in my hometown in a flat starting to slowly pick up a little. I was back on the dating scene and had two children who were slowly healing mentally after witnessing the previous few years of events. My brother was my rock and will always be that. He picked me up and helped us all to heal. However, life took another blow as my father passed away from a heart attack. This happened on the 27th of December 2004. My world fell apart, and I miss him every single day.

Due to those difficult few years, I felt a change was needed and I decided to relocate to North Wales with my new partner. We married and had another beautiful child, I started working at a women's mental health independent hospital which was fulfilling but obviously challenging and in a surprising twist of fate, I fell pregnant at the age of thirty-five and welcomed my beautiful fourth child.

My second marriage lasted a very long time, but then one thing led to another, and it sadly broke down. I tried to go through counselling to improve the situation, but things merely fell apart, and in the best interest for me and our children we decided it was best to go our separate ways.

In 2005 whilst walking I stumbled on a beautiful tree, I instantly connected with it. It was split down the middle but was somehow still growing and surviving. I decided to explore the tree and found a long piece that lay on the ground, and it became my safe space. Over the next few weeks and months, I visited the tree more and more as it became like a second home and somewhere I could be at peace. No matter what was going on in my life or whatever I was dealing with I could go to the tree and meditate and find inner peace and strength to deal with whatever life threw at me.

Shortly after my second divorce I visited the tree and it had been cut down and chopped back to the stump. I was heartbroken that my safe space had been destroyed. I was very emotional about this and decided to speak to the people who had cut the tree down and managed to secure some of the tree which I now have at my home permanently – the tree is now always with me. I still visit where the tree was, despite being chopped down, is growing again which is how I see my life. I have been repeatedly cut down, but I still grow and carry on moving forward.

During the second marriage I got into modelling which gave me enormous confidence and I continued doing this as a single parent and started to love the person that I was both physically and mentally. My first published photo was in a magazine called Fae magazine, thanks to the amazing Karen Kay; this became my reality, and I was so delighted. I had two more relationships that were quite toxic and didn't really benefit my mental health.

During my recovery I became an ambassador for a new crystal company called Spellbound.
Although I didn't know exactly what I wanted to do, I wanted to feed my passion and excitement, working with crystals. Becoming an ambassador for

Spellbound made me recognise how much I enjoyed crystals and their significance. This passion of mine was shared with a group and Lisa Williams helped me make it to reality, help me create a website, and in May 2023 Sunflower Moon Crystals became my new business and I started to rebuild my life. I wanted to show my children that even after all the storms I had faced I could still grow and move forward. Building my business has been an incredible journey, it has allowed me to show my children a new way of life. Everything I do is for them, I have seen them grow stronger and develop resilience and they make me so proud.

At the beginning of 2024 I became a grandmother for the second time to accompany my first grandchild. I really love how life has turned around, how I appreciate the incredible support and friendships I've made along the way. With special mentions to two special ladies in my life: Anni and Rachel, who have been tremendous pillars of support for me. I could not be the woman I am today without the two of these ladies in my life and they have supported me through all my decisions I have made in my life, since being in Wales.

A year after starting my own business, in May 2024, my business was growing, and I was nominated for a business award. Irrespective of whether I win or not to be selected as a finalist is a huge achievement and shows that I am being the businessperson I want to be.

In conclusion, we all have highs and lows in life, but the mindset and inner belief is something we can alter. We can achieve great things if we believe in ourselves, and I hope my journey resonates with you. You are not alone, and I have learned that we are strong enough to overcome any adversity.

I've been to the lowest points in life and come back up only to be thrown back down and pick myself up again and despite all the obstacles and challenges put in my way, just like my tree...

I'm still standing!

ABOUT THE AUTHOR

AMY IRELAND

Amy started her crystal business ten months after an accident in work which left her with memory lapse and some broken bones.

Amy built up a group which is now thriving and has helped her through her trauma, as she believes the crystals really helped to heal her too. This business feeds her passion, and she also now has time to focus on her four children and two grandchildren.

Amy has always loved nature and part of her journey started nineteen years ago when she used to visit a tree which to this day has inspired her every step of the way. Her tree was sadly chopped to a huge stump one year ago, but it is now growing new branches which has again made

Amy connect even more to this tree, as although it has been in a dark place and broken down, it now has started to grow again from all the trauma and it's thriving again.

New branches resemble Amy, broken then got back up and is growing stronger every single day, new beginnings, and a new chapter in her life.

Amy has pieces of her tree that she is carving into wands which will then be a reminder daily that even broken pieces can become beautiful things and Amy was always Amy, but she had to nurture and care for herself to then bloom into the courageous beautiful lady she is today, and her energy has heightened because she believes in herself again too.

You can reach Amy at:

www.facebook.com/groups/5817215478312827

ONE BREATH AT A TIME

By Amber Doughty

"Breathe. Allow love and intuition in." Sonia Choquette

My journey to self-trust began in a place of deep disconnection, shaped by a past that conditioned me to prioritise others' needs over my own. This conditioning took root in my early years when I assumed the role of an adult for my mother. Growing up too quickly, I learned to navigate the world through a lens of responsibility and care for others, believing that this was the essence of love.

In Australia where I headed off to travel and ended up living for a period of time, I found myself in a relationship that mirrored these early experiences. I didn't trust myself enough to question the lies and inconsistencies that became apparent over time. Instead, I accepted them, internalising the belief that enduring such dynamics was part of being loved. This relationship, much like my childhood, was a testament to the roles I felt compelled to play—roles that demanded self-sacrifice and a muted inner voice.

"Awakening is not changing who you are but discarding who you are not." – Deepak Chopra

Everything changed the moment I discovered I was carrying my daughter. Pregnancy brought with it a profound shift; it was as if the life growing inside me awakened a dormant sense of self-awareness and self-trust. I realised that I could no longer rely on anyone else for my well-being or that of my child—I had to rely on myself. This was just the beginning of my awakening.

The process was gradual but unmistakable. As I nurtured the life within me, I began to listen to myself more deeply than I ever had before. My intuition, which had been buried under years of self-neglect, started to surface. I knew that to provide the best for my child, I had to start by trusting myself and my instincts. This newfound clarity brought with it the strength to recognise and act upon the truths I had been avoiding.

"The magic in new beginnings is truly the most powerful of them all." – Josiyah Martin

Following the breakdown of my relationship, I returned home from Australia, seeking space to breathe and to focus on my role as a parent. I needed a sanctuary where I could nurture my child and myself, free from the chaos and emotional turmoil that had defined my recent past. My grandparents' home in France offered this sanctuary.

It was during my time in France that the full extent of my awakening began to unfold. One evening, as my close friend and I sat by the pool, chatting under the stars, I experienced a moment of profound clarity. The serene environment, combined with the supportive presence of my friend, allowed me to see the patterns that had kept me trapped for so long. I realised that my disconnection from myself stemmed from a lifetime of prioritising others' needs in a desperate attempt to feel loved.

"Sometimes, the bravest thing you can do is to break the cycle and create a new path." – Unknown

This revelation was both liberating and daunting. I understood that the cycle of self-neglect and external validation had not only shaped my life but had been a part of my family's narrative for possibly generations. But now, it was going to be different. I was determined to break these cycles, not just for myself but for my daughter. I wanted her to grow up knowing that true love starts from within, and that self-trust is the foundation of a fulfilling life.

Determined to find a different way, I embarked on a journey of self-discovery and healing. This journey led me to experiences and practices that would transform my life.

Discovering Unconditional Love and Coaching

In the process of redefining my life, I found love that was not conditioned on sacrificing my own needs. This love supported and encouraged my journey towards self-awareness and self-trust. It was a stark contrast to the relationships I had known before, offering a safe space for me to explore and embrace my true self.

A few years later, I also discovered coaching. This was a pivotal moment in my journey. Coaching raised my self-awareness, enabling me to identify and shift the limiting beliefs and behaviours that had held me back. It provided me with tools to shed the layers of conditioning that obscured my true self. With each session, I felt more empowered and in tune with my inner voice. I began to understand the importance of prioritising my own needs and the transformative power of self-trust. It was so impactful I followed an accredited path to become a coach myself and support others with this work.

"Your body is your first home: Breathing in, I arrive in my body. Breathing out, I am home." Thick Nhat Hanh.

While coaching played a significant role in my transformation, it was breathwork that truly felt like the missing piece of the puzzle. Breathwork introduced me to a profound sense of peace and self-trust that I had never experienced before. Through breathwork, I learned to navigate the chaos of the external world with a calm and centred inner state.

Breathwork allowed me to reconnect with my body and my inner wisdom. It taught me that no matter what was happening around me, I could always come home to myself through the power of my breath. This practice became a sanctuary, a place where I could find solace and clarity. It deepened my connection to myself and reinforced my belief that true trust and peace come from within.

Today, as I reflect on my journey, I am filled with gratitude for the experiences and insights that have shaped me. My path to self-trust has been one of awakening, healing, and transformation. It has taught me that self-trust is not a destination but a continuous journey—a practice of listening to and honouring my inner voice.

This work is bigger than us. It transcends individual experiences and has the power to create ripples of change across generations. I am excited to share the transformative power of breathwork and coaching, one breath at a time. Through my work, I hope to inspire others to embark on their own journeys of self-trust and to discover the profound peace and fulfilment that come from living in alignment with their true selves.

In sharing my story, I aim to offer a beacon of hope to those who feel disconnected and lost. Trusting oneself is a radical act of love and courage, and it is my hope that by sharing my journey, others will find the strength to embark on their own paths to self-trust and inner peace.

It is ALL possible.

As I draw a close on my chapter in this book, I invite you to take a moment to pause.

To take a breath with me. (Find a quiet spot, just for a few moments).

Sit comfortably, back straight or lie down, whichever you prefer.

Close your eyes.

Draw your attention to the breath.

Follow the journey of that breath.

Notice the temperature as it enters your nostrils.

Notice the journey it takes to fill your body, down to fill your lungs.

Notice how this breath feels as it enters & exits your nostrils.

Notice how it fills your entire body with life.

As your belly rises softly as you inhale.

With energy so powerful, it keeps you alive.

Notice your belly withdraw inwards as you exhale the breath with your body.

Notice any tension held in your body.

Now breath into that space.

Allow your breath to release that tension.

Ask yourself what is the weather on the inside today? How are you feeling? What do you need?

I invite you to follow this breathing exercise for the next week daily.

Notice how you feel after doing this each day.

Also, here are some journal prompts for you to dig a little deeper each day, take some time to reflect on each prompt. Come back to it after each daily breath.

Perhaps another layer will unravel.

Perhaps you will find more clarity and connection.

I would love to hear anything that comes up for you during your experiences or even offer further support if you feel this could be aligned for you. Connect via links as shared in my Bio.

1.Write about a time when you trusted your intuition and it led to a positive outcome. How did it feel to listen to and act on your inner guidance?

2. Describe a moment when you felt deeply connected to yourself. What were you doing, and what contributed to that feeling of connection?

3. What are some ways you can create space in your daily life to listen to your inner voice? How can you honour and prioritize what it tells you?

4. Identify a situation where you felt self-doubt. How can you reframe that experience to reinforce trust in yourself? What would you say to a friend going through the same situation?

5. List your core values. How do these values reflect in your daily decisions and actions? How can aligning more closely with these values help strengthen your self-trust?

6. Write about an area of your life where you've been ignoring your intuition. What is your intuition telling you about this situation, and how can you start to honour it?

7. Imagine your life five years from now where you fully trust yourself and your intuition. Describe what your life looks like. What steps can you take now to move towards that vision?

ABOUT THE AUTHOR

AMBER DOUGHTY

Amber Doughty BA (Hons)

Amber Doughty is a dedicated Home Ed Mum and an esteemed ACTP Coach, Influential Breathwork® Coach, and Breath Healing Release™ Practitioner based in the picturesque region of Cornwall. With a profound love for travel, all things spiritual, cooking, and nature—especially near the sea—Amber finds joy and inspiration in the world around her.

Amber's passion for personal development and spirituality fuels her reading obsession, driving her continuous growth and learning. Her professional background is rooted in education, and in the care sector, having studied to degree level and worked as an early year's teacher, manager, and trainer. As well as a Health and Wellbeing Coach in the Health Care sector before finding burnout forced her to make some big changes.

Breathwork has been a transformative force in Amber's life, fostering a deeper connection with herself, enhancing her self-trust, and reigniting her sense of purpose & improving her overall wellbeing. She believes this work transcends individual experiences, and she's excited to share its profound benefits, one breath at a time.

You can reach Amber at:

https://linktr.ee/amberdoughtybreathworkcoach

LINE IN THE SAND

By Rebecca Coe

As I sit on my sofa watching a re-run of a property programme from 2015, I realise just how much my life has changed over the past nine years. I was a veterinary nurse working in a large referral hospital as head theatre nurse, married, and a mum. I am now divorced and classed as disabled. I am no longer able to drive or work because my symptoms are so unpredictable. The only constant is my daughter and my dog, who keep me grounded and stop me spiralling into the pit of depression.

I was diagnosed with functional neurological disorder in 2018, after being rushed to hospital with a suspected stroke. I had no idea what was happening, with little recollection of those few days. Scans and blood tests came back normal and most of the neurological symptoms had gone. With little information I was discharged with a piece of paper that had a couple of websites written down. Little is known at what causes FND, like me the majority of patients are discharged with the same websites to look at and no follow up appointments.

After a couple of weeks off work, I returned to work in my role as head theatre nurse, working my normal hours. It soon became apparent that I struggled with the hours, the stress, the unpredictability of the days and the challenging environment. I still had very little help from medical professionals and could feel the black cloud of depression beginning to hang over me again. I had post-natal depression after having my daughter which I do not think ever left me. After numerous visits to the GP, I was finally referred to a neurologist to gain a better understanding of the condition and a treatment plan to help with the symptoms and the never-ending pain.

My mum and I left the consultation ninety minutes later a lot clearer. The neurologist diagnosed me with myalgic encephalitis, fibromyalgia, and hemiplegic migraines, which all come under the umbrella of FND. The neurologist advised me to begin thinking about my work situation, as realistically I would not be able to continue in the long-term. I had just been accepted for a degree in education studies, thinking I could go into teaching, but it was also classed as being a high pressurised career, however I was determined to finish and graduate.

Going back to work I tried to continue as normal, but this was becoming increasingly harder. As a manager I liked to lead by example, which I could no longer do. I decided to share my diagnosis with the rest of the team, thinking they would understand when I was unable to do a shift or be on call. I did not want any pity, but I did not expect the hostility I received. I saw the rolling of eyes and the odd moan when I physically could not continue. Not in my wildest dreams did I think my condition would be used against me, leading to my demotion for reasons I could not help. I was later told by an ex-employee that they were trying to replace me before my illness, asking staff on exit interviews if they were leaving because of me. I felt betrayed and angry, I could not trust anyone.

Looking back, had I had the energy I would have delved deeper into the reasoning behind it, as I do believe I was discriminated against. My mental state was also in tatters because of my husband's infidelity that year which resulted in him leaving, which we now also believe to be one of the catalysts of the FND.

Trying to continue working and facing the humility of my demotion, my degree and looking after my daughter began to take its toll. I began to develop new symptoms, one of which was dissociative episodes, I could hear people talking but could not respond. My parents were having to look after my daughter more and I knew deep down I could not continue so I took a position at a quieter practice. They were extremely understanding, from the start as I had taken the decision to explain about my condition during the second interview. They made reasonable adjustments for me and put various protocols in place for the patients and my own safety.

Six months after starting the job, COVID hit. Management took the decision for my safety to place me on furlough. It was during this time that I began journaling, partly to capture memories and the emotions in response to the horror COVID brought to so many families, but to also record my symptoms. It was journaling that helped me to realise that I had more good days than bad and I could not continue as I had been doing. I developed random tremors which at times could be quite violent. I lost count the number of times I threw a drink over myself or, more often than not my daughter and the dog.

Speaking to the managers on my return, about how I felt and how I was struggling, we mutually agreed dismissal on capability grounds was the best option. For the first time in twenty-four years of nursing I was unemployed. The first few weeks after leaving just felt like I was on annual leave, but then it hit. What was I going to do? I had to fill in form after form to get the necessary benefits, but I did not want to live on benefits. I wanted to work but could not. On the outside I was happy, trying direct sales but on the inside I was miserable. I was not a salesperson, and I was not happy.

Soon cracks began to show, the dark black cloud descended once again. Even though I had stopped working my symptoms were not getting any better. Any bit of stress, late night or illness triggered my symptoms. The random tremors became whole-body tremors and as soon as I sat down, I was asleep. What life did I have? I hated going out because of the unpredictability and lack of warning my symptoms gave me. I was in a pit of darkness and could not see a way out. I was a burden on my family and had very few friends because I no longer enjoyed socialising which people took personally, not understanding how I felt.

Because of the unpredictability of the illness, I was told to stop driving. I had never truly realised just how much I relied on my car. I was bought a mobility scooter to gain some independence, but I couldn't bear the sniggering, or comments being made. The nearest shop was a ten-minute walk which I could no longer do. I had to rely on my parents a lot, to go shopping and do the school runs. Again, I became a huge burden on them. They had recently retired, and they were having to look after me and Isabella instead of enjoying their retirement. I was miserable and felt like a drain on society. The same dark thoughts I had when I was first diagnosed with post-natal depression were creeping in. It was only the thought of leaving Isabella that pulled me through it and to seek professional help once again.

I had previously had cognitive behavioural therapy which seemed to help so I requested this again. I was told I had to have talking-therapy due to the lack of trained CBT therapists, so with this being my only option I gave it a go. The counselling did not go well. I am a private person who does not talk about emotions or how I am feeling. It did not help that the counsellor seemed disinterested, so after a few sessions I stopped.

It was not until I was scrolling through social media, I came across a lady who carried out distant crystal healing and reiki. I decided to give it a go as it had always interested me. I had previously had reiki treatment for a problem with my jaw joint and it worked amazingly well. During the first zoom session I immediately felt at ease and although I did not have a huge understanding of the processes, the practitioner released blockages which up until that point I did not realise I had, she also advised me what crystals I should have on me.

I had a couple of sessions and after each one I felt the dark cloud being lifted. I decided to look into taking a course in crystal healing to help me focus on something other than what was on TV. I had not realised just how in-depth the course would be. Luckily, it was self-paced so I could take my time. It was during this time I realised it was time to draw a line in the sand and to start looking at what I could do instead of what I used to do. I began shadow journaling, using prompts from oracle cards, practicing gratitude, and setting myself short term and long-term goals. I realised I could combine my knowledge in veterinary medicine and crystal healing to offer the additional therapy to animals as well as humans.

I am now a stronger, more determined person with an increased empathetic view to the struggles people face daily. Just because someone looks happy and healthy on the outside does not mean they are not struggling on the inside. As my mum has always taught me, treat people in the same manner as you would like to be treated. We do not know what they have going on in their lives and it could just take one positive comment to stop them doing something they might regret. Journaling and focusing on the positives are what get me through the day. Having a project to focus on helps a lot. I am now writing my own course combining crystal therapy and care of pets. It has been quite a journey and I still have bad days but during these days I look at my journal and see how far I have come and the obstacles I have had to overcome. Always try to turn a negative into a positive at least once during the day. It does help.

ABOUT THE AUTHOR

REBECCA COE

Rebecca is a single parent to a ten-year-old daughter and is a highly trained veterinary nurse. She was head theatre nurse at a large referral hospital and took additional courses to gain the advanced veterinary nurse diploma. In 2012 Rebecca found out she was pregnant with her husband, and after a difficult pregnancy Rebecca gave birth to a beautiful daughter. During the post-natal period Rebecca was diagnosed with post-natal depression for which she received talking therapy and medication. Abruptly in 2016 Rebecca's husband left after admitting to infidelity. She was also left in a considerable amount of debt after being told various bills hadn't been paid, contributing to the decision to move back to her hometown near her family.

In 2017 Rebecca suffered stroke like symptoms, resulting in being rushed to hospital. Here she was diagnosed with Functional Neurological Disorder, a disorder in which the electrical activity in the brain gets a little jumbled along with Fibromyalgia and Myalgic Encephalitis which are placed under this disorder. Very little is known about the disorder with many medical professionals having never heard of it.

Life has changed a huge amount for Rebecca since her diagnosis which has included having to stop a career she has wanted to do since being little and losing her independence. Rebecca is in the early stages of setting up her own crystal healing and pet bereavement business.

You can reach Rebecca at:

https://www.facebook.com/PreparingforRainbowBridge

FROM BREAKDOWN TO BREAK THROUGH

By Leigh-Anne Astley

As I sat in the back of my friend's car, tears streaming down my face, half of our belongings in bags squashed around us, I couldn't help but hate myself and the choices that I had made that led to this moment.

Clutching onto my upset babies sitting either side of me in floods of tears of their own, I had so many overwhelming emotions flooding over me. I felt like a failure, there was so much fear and uncertainty swirling around in my head that I couldn't think past the fog in my brain. The guilt inside of me weighed heavy, it felt like someone was taking blows to my stomach; it was physical and agonising, but I needed to take some accountability for the situation I was in.

I had invited an abusive, violent man and his drug addiction into our lives. He had come along at a time in my life when I was already in somewhat of an unstable mind frame, I had experienced a long-term relationship breakdown only six months prior. I was in a phase of 'finding myself.' My idea of finding myself at that time consisted of making the impulsive decision to come off all my medication that I had been taking for over fifteen years. The medication I was on controlled my bipolar disorder and ADHD. At that time, I wanted to come off them so that I could 'think straight,' yeah imagine the irony of that statement!

I have always been somewhat spiritual and alternative in my life and personality and so I made the decision that I wanted to take a more holistic approach to my mental health and wellbeing, so I just stopped. I made the impulsive and dangerous decision to bin all my anti-psychotics, mood stabilisers, anti-depressants and sleeping tablets. It was all going great for a few weeks, I was doing fine, or so my brain was telling me I was. That was when this new guy came on the scene, he liked to party, and he sold cocaine so for me it was company and a free supply. The fake high was replacing what my medication was no longer giving me and I fell deeper into its trap. I was on a dopamine high from a new sexual partner, drinking and putting class A substances up my nose four nights a week.

My mental health took a rapid decline, but I was so deep in it that I couldn't see it, nor could I see what he was doing to me. He moved himself into my apartment slowly over a month and it wasn't long before the aggressive outbursts started. Within a few weeks of living with me and my kids he became very manipulative about who I could speak to, he would take my phone out with him leaving me home with no way of reaching out to my friends or family. I was deeply unhappy and felt trapped in this situation with this guy who had changed towards me so rapidly once my roof was over his head. I initially didn't fear him physically hurting me or my children until one day when I confronted him about drugs. He had left them on my kitchen side right where my children would prepare their breakfast. Within minutes of me waking him to ask him to remove it he became very physically violent towards me; my eight-year-old daughter witnessed it all as she was flung to one side in an attempt to get him off me. He stormed out the flat as I was regaining consciousness and, in that moment, I knew I needed to get us all out of there! I called my cousin Casey, my friend Jaime and he flew down the motorway in his car to come and take me back to my hometown.

The next day as soon as my eyes opened, an overwhelming knot pulled heavy inside my stomach. I had done it; I had left, and we were safe. I shared joint custody with my children's fathers, and we stayed with my cousin to give me the respite to heal but my life was a mess for the months to follow. I neglected myself through further alcohol, substance abuse and casual sex. I was using it all to escape. I was receiving support at the time, and they all tried so hard to help me, but I wasn't being honest with myself never mind them. The people supporting me had no idea of the magnitude of the abuse I was doing to myself as_I hadn't disclosed that I'd been off my meds for months through fear of losing my children. I later moved into my best friend's home for a few months whilst I saved up. He lived alone so it gave me and the kids the safety and solace we needed. I worked hard on my mindset and saving up to find us a new place to call home.

I'd done it, I had begun rebuilding my life and I hadn't given up! I could have so easily but in every low moment I told myself to keep going, to keep fighting. Me and my children deserved a happy life, a safe life. I wanted so badly to be able to heal myself for them, they didn't ask to be born to a mum with mental illness and substance abuse issues. They deserved so much more than what I had put them through and the only way I could show them how sorry I was, was to change and create that safety for them by giving them the mum they needed. I had so much space during the time of my breakdown to sit and reflect and ask myself those all-important whys and some days it was soul destroying being so honest with myself but also so necessary for my growth.

After twelve months of courses and support my children were taken off child protection as I was proving that I could keep them safe. I was also trusting myself to make healthy and positive choices for us all. I took myself back to school to train to be a holistic therapist and alternative health practitioner to help better understand myself and learn new tools to help with my mental health and substance abuse recovery journey.

Alongside studying my diploma, I completed three years training as a Magdalene rose temple priestess which came with so much newfound knowledge, wisdom and understanding of myself. I wanted so much to help other women with the tools that I had used to heal myself and my own wounds along my healing journey and as if by magic I found a women's empowerment community online and I began to engage with the ladies who ran it. After a few months I approached them with a concept that I had previously had for a healing and wellness festival style event. It was inclusive to all budgets by getting other sisters in the community to come along and share their gifts as a collaboration event. As a practising witch in a small town, I had never had anyone to share my interests with before and I was over the moon to now be a part of a huge community of like-minded women all coming together to heal and grow and support one another. They were more than happy to join me in my vision and so Goddessfest was born.

It didn't last long as I was soon to discover that at the heart it wasn't what it professed to be and myself and other ladies in the community were made subject to some quite disturbing manipulative abuse and bullying, so we pulled away and formed our own community. Our women's community 'Queen Bees' is a safe space for women to heal, recover and grow whilst being held and supported by fiercely loyal sisters that are all on very different paths and stages of their own journey. I am grateful for that old group though as not only did it help me to recognise narcissistic abuse patterns, but it also made me establish and uphold my own personal boundaries. I met the love of my life my wife-to-be Louise in that community; she was one of the cofounders when I joined, and we always had such flirty chemistry between us. I also met some of my closest and most dear treasured sisters through that community.

I am a firm believer in everything happens for a reason and I truly believe it was fate as I would never have met Louise or had the opportunities it gave me, giving me the support, courage, and confidence to create and deliver Goddessfest. Our Queen bees were featured in a recent witchcraft documentary on channel four where I led an ancestral healing and land clearing ceremony on Pendle Hill with Suranne Jones. This was such an honour and the most surreal and powerful experience; it is one I will certainly never forget.

I have recently hosted my third successful Goddessfest wellness and empowerment weekender festival. Our women's community is thriving and I'm about to marry the woman that I love and adore, the one for whom I am eternally grateful for, the one of whom I will continue to grow and evolve with and share this crazy adventure called life with.

I truly believe that if I hadn't experienced all I have I would not have had the same fight and motivation for the life I have created for myself now. It took a few attempts to clean up my act, but it was worth the fight because I'm now happy in a stable and loving relationship. For the first time in my adult life, I can firmly say I am truly happy, I can say that I am proud of myself for not giving up in those moments of feeling broken. Today I sit and celebrate myself and every other woman out there who may have fallen on hard times but refuses to give up, I celebrate every woman fighting for themselves, their children and for every single woman out here reclaiming her innate power. I see you queen; you are loved, and you have got this.

ABOUT THE AUTHOR

LEIGH-ANNE ASTLEY

Leigh-Anne, a thirty-seven-year-old mum of two, Joshua seventeen and Elisse fourteen, began her healing and recover journey after years battling through mental illness, addiction, alcohol abuse and domestic violence. Leigh-Anne finally took control of her life when a domestic violence incident led to fleeing her home with her children leaving them homeless.

Leigh-Anne suffered a breakdown because of this, but little did she know the breakdown would lead to a major breakthrough. Leigh-Anne took herself back to school to qualify as a holistic therapist so that she could learn and navigate through her own recovery from mental illness and substance abuse. She studied her Magdalene rose temple priestess path for three years before her initiations and ordination which led her to deeper healing, growth, and transformation. Leigh-Anne wanted to help other women with the tools she has collected on her own personal journey, she created Goddessfest, a women's empowerment and wellbeing festival of which she has successfully hosted yearly for the past three years. She continues to support and empower women on their own healing and recovery journeys however that looks to them.

Leigh-Anne cofounded Queen Bees, a heart centred women's empowerment and recovery community with her partner in life Louise after the universe gave them a welcomed redirection. She has deep passion and commitment to providing a safe space for women to heal and grow whilst being held and supported by other women. Leigh-Anne continues to and evolve on her own journey whilst being in service to her community.

You can reach Leigh-Anne at:

https://www.facebook.com/share/g/2dRbn9qAavpkFU7B/

WITH WAVES OF GRIEF COMES HOPE.

By Anne-Marie Jones

Sitting down to write this chapter, has been the hardest thing I have ever done but I want to share how I went from being a shy, anxious girl with zero confidence, being bullied at school and not fitting in to being the woman I am today. It has not been an easy journey, but it has shaped who I am.

I was a young mum at seventeen years old. I believed the stereotype that my life was over, and I would never be anything other than a mum. Do not get me wrong, I love being a mum and would not change it, but it was hard and came with a lot of challenges. I had no confidence in myself and no ambition. As the boys got older, I started to feel like I wanted more for them. I started struggling with my health and was diagnosed with fibromyalgia. It made me feel useless and worthless as a mum. I was not able to do everything I used to, and everyday tasks were a struggle. I felt guilty that the boys were missing out on things because I was not as active.

At the end of 2015, I found my first MLM company and started to see what was possible. This is where I was first introduced to personal development and a book, 'The Secret' was recommended. This opened my eyes to the law of attraction. I was intrigued and started working on myself. I watched motivational videos on YouTube and started stepping out of my comfort zone. I began attending training events, which meant I had to get the train. This was something I'd not done before, and I really struggled with anxiety.

The biggest event I attended was a convention in London. I initially booked a train ticket but was too scared to go by train, so I sold my ticket, and a friend went out of her way and picked me up and we drove down to London together. Being in London away from my partner Dave and the boys for four days was hard. I had never been away from them for so long. I'm not a city girl and I love the countryside and a quiet life, so I felt overwhelmed with the huge crowds of people. However, I experienced things I had never done before, and despite being nerve-wracking, it was one of the best weekends.

A few months later, I fell pregnant and was excited for the future. At just seven weeks I suffered a miscarriage, that it completely broke me. I felt useless, my body was a failure and I sunk into depression. Then in March 2020, the world went into chaos. We found ourselves in lockdown, unable to go out and see family and friends; I was too scared to go out. Even Dave going to the supermarket would send me in a spin. I just could not cope. I was fixated on the news, following all the news stories. It consumed my life.

As things started to re-open, I was still very wary. I avoided certain places, especially places with lots of people and stayed home as much as possible. I stopped myself from watching the news and reading any articles and within a few weeks I was focusing my energy on the things I could control. I chose to go to places that were quieter and just tried to enjoy the time we had.

At the end of 2021 I had had enough. I did not want to live in fear anymore and I refused to limit me and my family anymore and so I went into 2022 with a positive attitude and one thing in mind. 2022 would be the year of positive change! Dave found himself a job, after being out of work for years to help care for me and the boys, due to my health. I was excited but also nervous about the change. I knew it was a positive move and we as a family would adjust. I started going out more, meeting new people and enjoying life and that was when I attended a workshop of Lisa's which really changed things. I was so nervous as I had never been to anything like it before but I left feeling absolutely amazing. This is where my spiritual journey really began.

I started following new people that inspired me. I listened and watched inspirational and motivational videos. My mindset was getting stronger.

Little did I know that my entire world was about to crash down, and everything would change forever. My mum had been poorly for some time, she had CROHNS and COPD for many years, but her health got worse beginning of 2022. We never expected to lose her the way we did. My world crumbled in seconds.

I still struggle with the trauma of the events that unfolded and I probably will for a while. I had two choices, crumble or be strong. Dave had just started training at his new job and the boys needed me. So strong was the only option I had but I did not feel strong at all. I felt lost, weak, vulnerable, and so sad. But every day I got up and did what I needed to do. Seeing how strong my dad was, helped to keep me going. It was not long after, we took dad for routine tests; to discover he had lung cancer. WHY? Had he not already been through enough? He now had to battle. Faced with a big operation, followed with chemotherapy, he literally just got on with things. He was my true hero, a real warrior.

Seeing the strength and resilience my dad had, helped keep us strong. But his fight was not enough and just eleven months after losing mum we had the heartache of losing dad too. I was numb. None of it felt real. Life really was unfair. Being the eldest girl, I felt I had to step up for my sisters and be strong for them. We had a funeral to arrange and a family home to empty. This was the hardest thing we had ever had to do. It was too soon after losing mum to have to go through all of that. Having to go through both my parents' personal possessions so soon did not feel right. I found it really difficult to let things go but me and my sisters did have a laugh at some things we found. Locking the door for the last time and handing the keys back felt like the end of an era. My heart ached. Those first few days after, I felt more lost than ever before. All those memories and years as a home, gone so quickly.

Everything that happened, has shown me that life is way too short. There are no guarantees, and anything could change at any time. I have made it my mission to do everything to make my parents proud. I used to speak to my dad a lot about the plans and ideas I had for the future. He was always so encouraging, supportive and gave good practical advice, which will always stay with me.

Over the eleven months after losing mum, me and dad became closer than we ever had. I loved going to his house and sitting down drinking tea watching the old soaps. It is one of the things I miss the most. He would always ask about my business and if I had found another shop yet or what events I had booked. I am so grateful that I got to spend so much time with my dad. I learned a lot from him. Seeing his strength, determination, and resilience, gave me the strength I needed.

After I lost mum, I turned to crystals and selfcare. Amethyst and opalite were the two crystals I used daily to bring calm and reduce the stress and anxiety. I joined Lisa's mastermind and met some amazing ladies that have become good friends as we support each other in business and personal life too. We are each other's cheerleaders.

Getting out and about, attending fayres was a good way to keep me distracted, whilst meeting new people which opened the doors to even more opportunities. While I did not fully believe in myself, I borrowed the belief from others to get me started and to push myself of that comfort zone and do things I really enjoyed. I still have moments of uncertainty, but I know I have the tools to help myself, whether that is by using crystals, meditating, breathwork, taking timeout with friends or family. I have learned that spending time to myself and focusing on my inner self has been paramount to my healing journey. Yes, I still have a long way to go on this journey of grief however, if it had not been for the tools I use, I most certainly would not be still standing.

Something I have learned is that looking after my own well-being is essential in being the best mum, wife, friend I can be. I used to always put myself last and feel guilty for any time I took for myself. Now I see that it is just as important to look after myself as it is to look after everyone else. It is true what they say, you cannot pour from an empty cup so, I consciously take time for me regularly, which has helped my anxiety, helped reduce my own stress and made me a happier person. Looking back, I hardly recognise the shy, anxious girl I once was. My journey has not been easy, but it has shaped who I am today.

We are now preparing for our rainbow baby to arrive, which has been the biggest blessing for our family after such a traumatic couple of years.

If I could give you one tip it would be to always trust your gut and never be afraid to go after what you want. Do not listen when people tell you that you cannot do something. I am proof that through hard work and determination you are capable of anything you wish. I have broken the stereotype of being a young mum that would never achieve anything in life and for that I feel proud.

Life will always throw things at us to test us, but it is how we choose to react that is important.

ABOUT THE AUTHOR

ANNE-MARIE JONES

Anne-Marie also known as the Well-Being Sister, is an advocate for women's wellbeing and self-care. Anne-Marie's mission is to help others prioritise their own well-being through self-care practices, the use of healing crystals, and the cultivation of self-love. She passionately believes in the importance of being true to oneself and maintaining a strong belief in one's own abilities and potential. Anne-Marie is a devoted mother of three boys, soon to be four, whose life experiences have profoundly shaped her journey and mission.

In late 2015, amidst the challenges of managing fibromyalgia, Anne-Marie began her entrepreneurial path, seeking both personal fulfilment and a way to improve her well-being.

This led her to the world of personal development, where she found the tools and inspiration to transform her life.

Anne-Marie lost both her parents within twelve months of each other, instead of falling Anne-Marie used her pain and ignited a drive within her to push beyond her comfort zone and live her life with purpose and passion. Anne-Marie has always been committed to community and support. She has co-hosted numerous events to uplift local small businesses and successfully opened two pop-up shops, creating spaces for connection and growth within her community. Anne-Marie treasures moments spent in nature, finding peace and rejuvenation in the beauty of scenic views.

Anne-Marie's journey is one of resilience, growth, and unwavering self-belief. Through her work and personal story, she continues to inspire others to embrace their well-being.

You can reach Anne-Marie at:

https://linktr.ee/annemariejones

THE MOMENT OF CLARITY

By Johanna Lunney

This is a story about a courageous girl who transformed into a woman and survived by never giving up.

I was diagnosed with ADHD at the ripe old age of forty-nine, I was shocked and in disbelief. I didn't understand how I could have the 'naughty boy syndrome.' I had always believed that I was just one of life's strugglers, a nightmare, a drain on society, I didn't have ADHD. However, when they were explaining ADHD to me, it was like a tick box in my head of matching those ADHD traits and my life. Everything they said made sense and wow a weight had been lifted. I no longer wanted God to take me away in my sleep, I felt like I now had the rest of my life to love, have fun and bring my dreams – with a few tweaks, into reality.

After a lot of deep research into ADHD, I realised that I had hated myself most of my life for no reason, I just have a different brain and to be honest I really like the things it has to offer and if I can find a way to manage the bad side, I'll be a very happy human.

Now let's go deep and dark, this is a snippet of life as a woman with undiagnosed ADHD.

From an early age the self-hatred and masking began, it was slow but consistent, self-talk of self-hate, names I would call myself, idiot, lazy, messy and thicko. Other people would call me a dolly day dreamer, a class clown and clumsy. Teachers would tell me that I could be clever if I just tried, they didn't understand that I was trying. People told me that I would be good to hire out for sad occasions because I was super sensitive and emotional. I was always berating myself as I felt like a bad person and couldn't understand why I couldn't get my shit together, like everyone else.

Growing up I somehow managed to wing it through life with many lows and highs, yet still managing to raise three amazing kids. I also had numerous business and job ideas, one time I decided I was going to be the next best DJ, so I borrowed the money and off I went to buy my first set of technic 12 10's. This was going to be the best job ever, the kids would be proud, we could travel the world together, buy our own house, this was it. Finally, I was so bloody excited but then my pathetic person had other ideas, one lesson in and three days later it was over, the decks become an add on to the floordrobe for a few years then disappeared to die in the garage.

In my early forties, the perimenopause started to kick in with its metal toe capped boots. I was struggling more than ever, especially with my emotions, sleep, body tremors, soaking hot sweats at night and memory. My self-talk turned up a thousand decibels and my negative thoughts amplified. I felt that I was a burden to everyone and was convinced I was giving the kids a shit life and every day wondered 'why did I wake up?' The debilitating pressure of knowing I had to make decisions and fearing I'd make bad choices was overwhelming, but every day I would stick on a happy mask and off I'd go to unintentionally shit on everyone's day.

In January 2019 a horrendous new journey began, after thirteen years I caught my partner having an affair. It's not so much the affair but the lies and deceitfulness which destroys you physically and mentally. It's the intense pain you feel for your children, knowing they are hurting too, which rips your soul apart. Meanwhile, time does not stop to let you heal or adjust to your new normal, it just keeps going.

During the next four years, this became even more apparent with some of my friends, as they did not feel like I was moving on as quickly as they thought was appropriate. I felt like I was failing my friends and family as I was no longer able to put on my mask to be the happy persona they were used to. I felt like I was drowning, and things just kept getting worse. I was sexually assaulted by someone I had trusted, I lost good friends and wanted to die. The only thing keeping me alive was how my children would be affected. I focused on things like how, I'd already given my children a rotten life and that the last thing they needed was to be grief stricken for the rest of theirs. These thoughts were constantly in my head, and I knew that I needed to get out of the deep dark pit.

One really bad day I phoned the mental health unit. I was very vulnerable and emotional but whatever I said they gave me an appointment two days later. I didn't know what to expect or what even they could do as I'd been on prozac since I was sixteen and had begged for help before, but I just needed to stop the intense sadness and busyness in my head. I knew that I needed some peace and then maybe I could be a good mum to my kids and the best nanna to my beautiful granddaughter. What happened in that hour and half meeting at Hafod changed my life for the better forever, I finally had an answer, it was ADHD.

Fast forward to medication day and oh my goodness, gradually the thoughts just drifted away like grey clouds. Next thing I knew, I was up cleaning and sorting, I had so much to do. I don't mean we lived in a shithole, but I did text all the kids apologising and thanking them for loving me unconditionally and not calling social services. I have also realised that it's not appropriate to offer toast and cereal as a balanced diet, so again I thank God from the bottom of my heart for my beautiful friends, who I now know have genuinely liked and loved me.

As the weeks and months rolled by the medication helped and apparently, I have been very lucky to have no horrible side effects and the ones I do have, don't outweigh the good I get from them.

Since being diagnosed with ADHD I have learned so much about it and myself. I know now that my anxiety and extreme fear of failure and rejection is linked to ADHD, it even has a name – rejection sensitive dysphoria. I have also learned how putting on a daily happy-go-lucky persona, isn't what everyone else does and is in fact masking. I remember a conversation I had with my eldest when she was a teenager, we were talking about her anxiety, how she felt like every day she was acting and how much energy it took out of her to pretend. Acting like she wasn't nervous, uneasy, worried and had no confidence. I remember telling her that it was normal, that we all, 'fake it until we make it,' I now know that this isn't the case, both of us were masking.

I'm learning to be understanding, accepting and, very lovingly trying to forgive myself. Looking back, it's really hard to believe I hated myself so much and how this had a ripple effect on my loved ones. My self-hatred has hurt my family and caused me to miss out on so many opportunities. I've struggled with impulsive buying and faced my financial difficulties. Thousands of pounds, especially in parking fines, missed and late payments, all ignored, adding to feelings of shame, embarrassment, and stress. It was just too overwhelming to acknowledge the financial difficulty that I kept finding myself in and I would just put the unopened letters into the magic drawer where they did not exist. At least not in my head.

Sometimes I do get those pangs of hurt when I think how life could have been different for us but that gets me nowhere and wastes more precious time. So, I pull up my big girl pants and I remember how grateful and thankful I am for my three beautiful children, who I love and adore, who have saved my life, on more than one occasion, by never giving up on me and now to be blessed with our little warrior, my beautiful grandchild.

Even though it's been a tough life in many areas I have also had some of the most amazing, funniest times of my life filled with so much love. My daily struggles haven't completely disappeared, but life has got easier now that I have understanding and support around me.

So, to the future, with the help of my medication, the knowledge I'm gaining and have collected throughout life, the love in my heart and the hope to help make the world a beautiful place to be... I'm on a mission to find the best types of strategies, anything to help us neuro-spicys live our best lives in harmony with the not-so-spicys, because actually, we all need each other.

Dedicated to my dad with love and forgiveness.

ABOUT THE AUTHOR

JOHANNA LUNNEY

Johanna is a trained beautician, Johanna specialises in massage therapy, reflexology and lymphatic treatments, for the last 25 years Johanna has been making her clients feel amazing and giving them that relaxation experience.

At 49 years old Johanna got diagnosed with ADHD, this turned her world upside down and is now learning to navigate through a new lens.

Johanna is mother to three fabulous children and Nanna to her miracle grandchild.

Johanna's dream is to have a farm retreat, which will be a safe space for clients to come and escape from the world, to relax and be at ease with nature allowing them to regenerate.

You can reach Johanna at:

https://www.facebook.com/beautyby.johannalunney

CURVEBALLS AND COMEBACKS: LIFE BEYOND THE CHAIR

By Sarah Clarke-Lees

For as long as I can remember, I was Sarah the hairdresser, transforming lives one haircut at a time, until life threw me an unexpected curveball. My story isn't about hitting rock bottom and crawling out. It's about being at the top and having to start again. No one talks about that – the shame attached to, 'My life was amazing, then something shitty happened, so I made a new amazing life,' so this is how the old me became the new me.

From leaving school, I worked in a salon, learning my craft through an apprenticeship. By sixteen, I was spending over forty hours a week, often more, in a salon. Hairdressing was a huge part of my identity. There's no feeling quite like having someone tell you that you've made their day, boosted their confidence, or created something that makes them feel better about themselves. Clients share so much when they sit in your chair – engagements, weddings, pregnancies, break-ups, divorces, losses. You're trusted with their self-esteem, confidence, and secrets. Some days, you can visibly see the weight lift off their shoulders when you nail the cut and colour they've dreamed of, transforming them into the version they want to be. You're part of their special moments – graduations, promotions, weddings. Your advice matters.

It can be incredibly sad too. I've cried with clients, cried at home after heavy days, and sobbed in the staff room out of frustration or sadness. But I've also laughed until I couldn't breathe, with tears streaming down my face. I've smiled as families and friends admired their loved ones' new looks, partners started flirting, and children were amazed. It's the best job in the world.

There's a selfish side too. I get to be creative all day, every day. I have conversations with a variety of people, hear music and chatter, and wear clothes I like. I work with mates, go to events, see shows, and immerse myself in creativity and art. I get a pat on the back every few hours when someone says, "Thank you, I love it," or "I feel so much better now." What other job gives you such regular job satisfaction?

I loved it so much that I started teaching hairdressing. Then I moved up to a creative team, becoming the person on stage with the mic, showing huge audiences what I'd created. I was living my wildest dreams – travelling, staying in beautiful locations, meeting new people, enjoying the glitz and glamour.

Then it wasn't incredible anymore. I started aching when I got home. I'd drop my comb a lot and my hands were so stiff that in the morning I'd cry. I had pins and needles, sharp pains, and dead arms. I didn't know what I would do or how I could stop it.

Convincing my GP that it wasn't weight-related was the first hurdle. The second was finding out the cause and articulating the symptoms. Several hospital visits later, a consultant told me, "We feel it is work-related and suggest you think about giving up hairdressing and have a change of career."

I felt sick. I shrieked, "Oh well, you can't be a consultant anymore, what are you going to do?" He didn't know me or my situation, yet he was ready to tell me to leave hairdressing just as I was achieving my dreams.

I couldn't accept that this was my life. After a painful procedure on my right arm, I knew it wasn't a cure, but it bought me some time. My workplace was amazing, listening to my triggers and ensuring I had help. My clients allowed extra time and additional stylists to assist me. I found a new normal.

Five years later, I was still doing shows, photo shoots, and seminars. I'd continued to run classes and was still living my dream but secretly, I've been waking up with no feeling in my arms or hands. I was nervous about holding babies, unable to pull clothes out of the washing machine or change bed sheets and I couldn't play with the kids or even wash my own hair. I was exhausted.

How did I create a new dream? How did I pick a new normal for me? Was I ready to give this up? I'm a glass-half-full kind of person, but this time, I couldn't see how it would end well. I was sad, going to work with a smile, helping others while sinking deeper into anger. No one was solving my problems.

I didn't want to be around people outside of work; it was too draining. I resented listening to others because I was giving an optimistic version of my reality. The hardest part was knowing others had it worse, people with life-threatening illnesses or missing limbs were climbing mountains and so the guilt I felt every time I felt sorry for myself was overwhelming.

I knew I had to do something. I stopped working in the salon, which was the hardest thing I've ever done. Saying goodbye to my work family, clients who became friends, and the local businesses was heart-breaking. I couldn't visit the salon after I left, though I promised I would.

I continued in education, on stages, and in studios, but eight months later, I knew I couldn't wake up alone in hotels with dead arms anymore. I needed to stop. This was my final goodbye to Sarah the hairdresser, to the life I'd worked so hard to build.

I thought about the other aspects of my job. What could I do that kept me in a creative environment without the physical strain? That's when 'That Alternative' was born. Thinking about the things I loved about my successful career in hairdressing and how I could make those elements work in my new career, the space was born. A creative hub with a photography studio, hair room, and hotdesking space. A place to be around creatives, work with creatives, and be a creative.

It's still weird that people in my new working life don't know I used to do hair, that I was on stage talking about hair. They know me as a studio owner, someone who runs a space they use. The new me, shaped by the old me, with resilience and grit, refusing to give up.

The guilt and mental torture of grieving my old life and welcoming a new one is massive. I don't publicly show the struggle, just the next stage. I've lost my identity and am still figuring out my new one, but I know I won't give in. I'm grateful for each new experience that brings me joy, and the new opportunities are slowly becoming my favourites.

If you ever feel you're losing your identity, remember sometimes life throws you a curveball, and you've got to swing for the fences. Embrace the chaos, dig deep for that grit, and create something new and brilliant out of the mess.

You've got this, just like I have.

ABOUT THE AUTHOR

SARAH CLARKE-LEES

Sarah is an entrepreneur and mentor based in Blackpool who has navigated the challenging waters of career change to find a new identity that resonates with her passions. Originally rooted in the world of hairdressing and education, Sarah's journey is a testament to the power of embracing change and reinventing oneself.

After years of success in the hairdressing industry, Sarah had to explore new horizons. This led her to create That Alternative Studio and That Alternative HQ spaces that not only serve the creative community but also embody her own journey of transformation. The studio and co-working space are reflections of her belief that change, though often daunting, can lead to the most fulfilling chapters of our lives.

Sarah's story is one of resilience and adaptability. Her transition from hairdressing to entrepreneurship wasn't just a career shift; it was a complete redefinition of her identity. Through mentoring and coaching, she now shares her insights on embracing change with others who are navigating similar paths. Sarah encourages those she mentors to see change not as an obstacle, but as an opportunity to discover new strengths and passions.

With a passion for helping others and a keen understanding of the challenges that come with change, Sarah is dedicated to inspiring and guiding others as they carve out their own unique paths in life.

You can reach Sarah at:

https://www.instagram.com/thatalternativestudio/

UNDERSTANDING NARCISSISM

By Nergus Saddique

I'm a practicing narcissistic relationship coach, I help many individuals with their narcissistic relationships. Having experienced narcissism all my life, I can now see and recognise this in a position of power. Narcissistic personality disorder is a mental health condition, in which people need and seek much more attention, they want people to admire them, they may lack empathy and have a high sense of their own importance. I have the privilege of working with vulnerable families and children in care. In some of these cases I'm able to help families recognise red flags in narcissism.

Growing up amongst my siblings I had to behave a certain way around them. I often found this confusing as watching my friends growing up in their households with their siblings and parents who appeared to be happy, left me envying their relationships and questioning why my relationships with certain family members were different. I was far too young to understand what I know today, and that is I was in multiple narcissistic relationships.

In childhood we all had nicknames, Piggy was mine, I felt mine was the worst out of the lot, Piggy came about because my siblings thought I was fat and ugly, this made me feel awful about myself.

As the years progressed into my teenage years my confidence in myself began to completely disappear, I lost weight and had got taller, so Piggy felt less offensive by now, however some of my siblings began to find other ways to bring me down such as questioning and comparing my educational abilities. I was left feeling not capable; my sister constantly reminded me that education wasn't for me. Feeling suppressed over the years this had a huge impact on my academics. I remember my sister telling me that I would make a great housewife, and I should stay focused on that. I began to adopt her idea, even though I knew this was not what I wanted, I felt my thoughts were being controlled and leaving me to feel trapped. I was scared to use my voice to describe my feelings as I didn't want to be made fun of. With mum being absent and having our cultural differences she had no idea how I was feeling, she was occupied creating a status for herself in society. During those years I felt very lonely.

When I reached twenty, I met my husband, I felt I had some sense of freedom. He would listen and respect me, I knew my opinion mattered when around him, all of this of course felt very unnatural at the time, I was never used to having anyone allowing me to have an opinion or show me love. The only love and affection I had ever received was from my dad, my brothers often allowed me to express the way I would feel without judging me. With all this new profound freedom I was unsure how safe it was to use it; it took years for me to embrace my new life.

After so many turbulent years with my family members, when our angelic daughter was born, she brought me peace and harmony and soon after our little warrior followed, bringing me strength and power. The birth of our children made a huge impact on the way I wanted to live my life and find ways to protect them. Without realising I began to put boundaries in place, this impacted my siblings and mum losing control over me. My mum and sisters were enraged by my new way of living and took a drastic decision to cut me out of their lives. I needed to understand why they felt so strongly to break contact not just with me but with my husband and children too, I needed answers as to why they'd smeared me to other family members.

The first few years of their sudden departure left me feeling angry, sad, lonely, and massively confused. As I looked for answers I decided to study human behaviours, I came across narcissism, I was keen to learn more after realising how too familiar it had sounded to me. Reliving my years at home I remembered how I would avoid confrontation, as I was constantly fighting a losing battle, I couldn't put a point across, as my siblings and mum felt I had no value. I found ways to cope over those difficult confrontations by diverting intense conversations and remaining calm, I'd always show compassion by listening and supporting my mum and sisters to find solutions, but once I had set my own boundaries this had pushed them away. Narcissistic people cannot cope with boundaries, they feel entitled.

The more I learnt about narcissistic traits I realised that my family members had displayed these for years, such as the need of superiority and wanting to be admired or the desperate need of being praised, they would show grandiose behaviours and arrogance there were fantasies about their personal power and intelligence, they would show exaggerated feelings and have random outburst, they'd show no empathy, they'd be envious of others or them thinking that others were envious of them, everything had begun to make sense.

After studying their behaviours, I became more aware of my own behaviours. It was clear that my mum and sisters would not change and that the change had to come from me, I had taken steps by showing less interest in boosting their egos, I stood my ground with confidence and learned to say no, I'd refuse to argue by walking away and disengaging, I learnt that this hadn't meant that I lost an argument it meant there was no compromising with them.

During this period the stress had taken a toll on my health and narcissistic abuse can leave you with many health problems. I have developed trust issues I struggle with insomnia and anxiety; I have severe stomach problems. I was worried that my children were becoming my carers, so I had to take back the control. I learned to be kind to my inner child; I'd regularly speak to her and remind her that she had permission to live her life the way she wanted to without being controlled or judged. I took support through therapy with my own mental health, this helped me to find strategies to manage my levels of stress by beginning to journal my feelings about all the hurt and pain my family had caused me. I would use meditation as an escapism and surround myself with likeminded people.

Making the change in my own behaviours and gaining the knowledge around narcissism has helped and allowed me to understand different types of narcissism and their traits. It was key that I understood the behaviours of my family members, as I'm now able to move on knowing that I served my mum and sisters as the best version of me. This had made me realise the knowledge I had gained had given me the power to make peace with myself and help others who are in a similar situation.

Life after narcissism sent me on my spiritual journey, listening to the universe and looking out for signs has helped me to embrace change. I have learned not to trust my fears now that I know my strength. I'm much more careful with whom I'm exchanging my energies with. I've had to teach myself self-worth, and its importance as this is something I hadn't been taught, showing kindness to myself by running a bath or spending hours drawing or reading without feeling the guilt or shame for not doing house chores instead, has helped me to raise my own self-worth. I have also learned to be comfortable with setting goals for myself and manifesting them, this has helped me with my self-belief around being able to achieve whatever I wish to set out to do. It's normal for me to have doubts or find myself running back into my dark past, as long as I'm not there for too long, fortunately my loved ones are never too far behind, they always remind me of the light that I had found at the end of the tunnel. I show gratitude to the universe and to my guardian angels for guiding me for the journey my life has been on and the direction it continues to take.

Having the knowledge and power has made me an expert in working and understanding my clients who are in narcissistic relationships. I have helped and supported many people to recognise narcissistic traits and how to deal with a narcissists. I hold workshops to make people aware of narcissism and the physical impact it leaves on them.

Without my mum and sisters, I wouldn't be the empowering woman I have become today, I'm so thankful to my father and brothers for giving me the normality whilst growing up as I'm not exactly sure where I'd be.

I'm thankful to my little people, they gave me strength and power to use my voice, to reclaim back my life and find peace.

I'm thankful to my kind and generous husband for coming into my life at the time where I felt I wanted to give up, making me visible and showing me that I mattered and still do and supporting me in everything I do.

ABOUT THE AUTHOR

NERGUS SADDIQUE

Nergus is an accredited Coach. She is also the founder of Life Amongst Narcissist. Nergus has worked and supported many individuals, families and young people for over 20 years through their relationships, she has helped them understand and manage their overwhelming emotions and to live their life's more balanced and Intune with their emotional waves.

Following her own turning point, Nergus decided it was time to create a safe space and inspirational space for clients with their awareness and their healing process. She helps them to rediscover their personal growth and their true purpose.

Nergus works with clients to understand narcissism and the different types of narcissism. She helps recognise red flags, and how to manage a narcissist. She also helps with how to create inner peace whilst in their narcissistic relationships.

With a background in adult teaching and working in Social Care she has spent the past 10 years working with vulnerable adults, families and young people with housing difficulties, addiction, parenting and poor mental health.

Nergus works with clients online and offline by acknowledging and supporting their experiences and feelings, she shares the importance of boundaries and to actively bring the focus back on themselves.

You can reach Nergus at:
https://www.facebook.com/profile.php?id=100086470478827

THE UNIVERSE HAD MY BACK

By Louisa Herridge

At age twenty-five, I was at the top of the Sydney Harbour Bridge – a climb that everything inside me told me I couldn't do. I already had such limiting beliefs telling me that I couldn't do it. I didn't have a fear of heights but as I climbed that bridge, the terror gripped me, my inner demons told me I couldn't do it, but I dug deep and knew that it was just my inner voice trying to stop me.

The euphoria of reaching that highest point lives with me now and although, over the years, my inner demon has got the better of me, I have always known deep down that I could achieve anything that I set my mind to. I knew that I could achieve anything in life.

The fears that were stopping me climbing that bridge were the same limiting beliefs that stopped me following my career dreams and stopped me going for what I wanted in life. I always wanted to be a writer, a journalist or work in television but my plans were derailed by chronic back pain and surgery. Whilst living with that insidious pain, my life took a different plan and I trained to be an English teacher. For sixteen years I followed a profession that I had never set out to be in however, I loved teaching, and I was good at it, but in 2019 my life took another turn, and the universe gave me a nudge back in the right direction.

My journey into setting up my own business during the pandemic started by sharing my story. I shared parts of my story on social media and then joined a book collaboration. Here is the crazy thing... I didn't dare to tell anyone. I was an English teacher, and I was terrified to tell people that I was going to be a published author. That inner demon was back and trying to hold me back.

Fast forward four years and I am now a four times best-selling author and a writing coach helping women to tap into the power of their stories, to write and publish. I am also privileged to have been the editor for this collaboration and been part of the planning process using to my *Storytelling for Success* method. This method is underpinned by positive psychology and is about tapping into your limiting beliefs, your adversity and exploring the power that you have by editing, interpreting, and retelling your story, your way.

Sometimes in life when bad things happen, we tell our stories with the adversity as the headline of the story. However, if we edit the story then we reframe and change how we tell it, the edit allows us to look at what we have achieved, received, or gained despite the challenge or trauma. It is the grit, the resilience, and the power that we need to talk about but sometimes we must work hard to find the edit or reframe trauma.

When I first began to share my story, what was very hard to admit, to myself firstly, and then publicly, was that I had been a victim of two abusive relationships. I married the perfect man who turned out to be a nightmare. The mask slipped and I finally saw him for what he was. His coercive control was wrapped around me, so when I was away from him talking to other people I could see the lies, but as soon as I was with him the fog descended and I couldn't think for myself and his sincere declarations of love and how much he needed me put me back under his spell.

As I emerged from the chrysalis of my broken marriage, I realised the mental abuse that I had been living with. The confidence that I had lost. My counsellor was guiding me to find myself, to work on my self-esteem and to love myself first, but sadly, back then I thought I knew best. My broken pieces couldn't be fixed by myself alone. I needed someone else to pick up the pieces, to fix me and tell me that everything would be okay.

Within a few months I'd met someone the opposite to my ex-husband but what was glaringly the same was my vulnerability, my low self-worth, and the people pleaser in me who was desperate to fix someone else too. We were the perfect match. I had found the validation that I still needed and to heal the wounds that were still open, I plastered them with this new love story whilst ignoring the red flags.

Fast forward five years and I was a single mum, again licking the wounds of a second destructive relationship and above all blaming myself for everything and feeling so much guilt. My counsellor five years earlier had urged me to 'love myself first' before starting a new relationship but I didn't listen at the time, or maybe I couldn't. I had yet again been a victim of abuse – emotionally, mentally, verbally, and physically. Yet as a strong, educated, and confident woman, it took another two years before I could fully say out loud that I was a victim of abuse.

The guilt and the blame that I felt when I left this second relationship were because I felt like I had made all the same mistakes, so of course it was my fault. This is where I need to edit that story. I can remember how I felt and can see how much healing I needed but I wasn't ready. I was blaming myself when in fact I was doing the best I could at the time with the tools that I had in a very toxic environment. I wasn't to blame for the manipulation and deceit, and it was carrying that blame the first-time round that meant that my self-worth and self-esteem were chipped away even more. My edit of this story is that after both relationships I had the grit and determination to leave and to start again. I was able to tell people and to ask for help and eventually I found the acceptance so that I could begin to heal.

I left the relationship in July 2017 when my daughter was two, and the next two years were harder than the time that we were together, due to what I now know is a trauma bond. He was inextricably in my life, and I carried the guilt of breaking up the family unit.

In June 2019, life as I knew it changed when he physically assaulted me. When the police interviewed me realisations of years of physical, emotional, and verbal abuse unfolded. He was charged and pleaded guilty to *Assault with battery,* which, in a subsequent law change could have been *Non-fatal Strangulation,* and family court found twelve cases of *Physical, Emotional and Verbal Abuse* to be *Fact.*

Ten months of court hanging over me took its toll and in February 2020 what would become my first round of family court was over. After the intense, all-consuming adrenaline of court and the result, I was left deflated. A hopeless balloon with no life left. For the next week I was absent. I lay on the sofa for days and nights on end. I was trapped in waking sleep and suffocated by my own thoughts. Only getting into some semblance of dress to do the school run. I was broken. It had broken me but again this is the wrong story. It didn't break me. I wasn't broken, but for such a long time telling this version of the story felt like I was in control. By telling people that I had 'a breakdown' and came through it stronger made me feel strong and I thrived knowing that my story was inspiring others, but the true power of the story is what happened after.

I didn't break. I reached a point where I was emotionally and physically burnt out, but I had the power to grow. I had the grit and determination to be more and to want more. I had the resilience to say 'no' to the inner demons and to put things in place so that I could rise.

Slowly, I began to rebuild my strength and during more therapy, I began to take control of my own vision and my own future. After being off work for so long, something had shifted in me. The career driven teacher realised that it was okay to not be a full-time teacher with a responsibility; always striving for the next promotion, sending my daughter to breakfast club and afterschool club, spending weekends and evenings marking, hearing my daughter say, *'You love marking more than me,'* missing her assemblies, and class open days.

It was during a therapy session that I realised that nobody was forcing me to be a teacher and that just because I had spent sixteen years of my life teaching, it didn't mean that I had to stick to the plan. I decided that I was going to turn my adversity into positivity and start my own business. I just didn't have a clue how!

I was still consumed with negative thoughts and without much understanding, would openly declare that the universe hated me, yet I wasn't doing anything to show love or respect to the universe. There was a pinnacle moment where this began to change. As I lay on the sofa in a vortex of doom day after day, I began to listen to 'The Secret' and for the first time, I was introduced to *The Law of Attraction*. A few days later I was invited to a vision board session – I didn't know but the universe was already responding.

I reluctantly went along; it was a chance to escape the house that had become my prison as I'd been off sick for three months. As I listened to the speaker talk about her triumph over adversity and how the law of attraction had changed her life, I sobbed. Every word resonated with me. From within the depths of my anguish and despair, a spark flickered and there was a shift.

I sat in a booth on my own and created my very first vision board. I put my intentions down and as they became goals, I began to see real visions of my future. I also reignited a spark that had long been forgotten, my true passion of writing as I put on the board *best-selling author*. I felt it in my soul, and I left the session a different person.

Twelve months later, every vision on my board had become a reality including setting up a business, new home, and best-selling author. The universe and I have been firm friends ever since.

My journey started with sharing my story and now my purpose is to help others to share theirs. I think the universe had my back all along.

ABOUT THE AUTHOR

LOUISA HERRIDGE

Louisa Herridge, The Storytelling for Success Coach, is a four-times best-selling author and TEDx speaker. She is a passionate and empowering coach who inspires and supports women to find their own power and success through using their story in business, books and beyond.

Louisa does this by helping women to build their businesses by using her *Storytelling for Success* method to create inspiring and authentic content by tapping into their meaning and purpose and using their story as a superpower to connect with their ideal clients.

She also leads The Publishing Pod alongside her partner Jo Wildsmith, and works with authors to support them in planning, writing, and publishing their business non-fiction books.

Louisa is known as the Queen of Collaborations and has curated three best-selling book collaboration books within her own business and now partners with other business owners to lead their own collaboration book to create an asset for their own business.

Louisa is a proud mum to Emilie aged nine and they are both members of a local Amateur Dramatic society and love performing in musicals together. Louisa loves to travel and is a Disney fanatic! Louisa is a lover of people and loves nothing more than connecting and networking with like-minded women.

You can reach Louisa at:

www.louisaherridge.co.uk

ACKNOWLEDGEMENTS

I would like to dedicate this book to all those women who have felt alone, struggled or held themselves back.

This book is to give you the determination to push through those boundaries and become the future self you have always dreamt of.

I would also like to dedicate this book to the incredible 28 women who have shared their story to help you, the reader. Their words are now on these pages to give hope and positivity into the world. Congratulations.

I would like to thank you the reader for choosing this book, for believing in these incredible women. I hope this book brings you joy and positivity into your life as you continue your life's journey.

REFERENCES AND CREDITS

Front cover design – Designed by the host Lisa Williams.

Proof and editing – Louisa Herridge
https://www.facebook.com/louisaherridgecoach

Formatting – By the host Lisa Williams

Published – By the host Lisa Williams

www.lisawilliams-lmg.co.uk

STAY IN TOUCH

Please scan the QR code to connect with the author Lisa, you can follow this link.
https://www.lisawilliams-lmg.co.uk/contact

Printed in Great Britain
by Amazon

50511891R00149